The Power of
**Verbal
Intelligence**

The Power of
Verbal
Intelligence

Tony Buzan

Thorsons
An Imprint of HarperCollins*Publishers*
77–85 Fulham Palace Road
Hammersmith, London W6 8JB

The website address is: www.thorsonselement.com

and *Thorsons* are registered trademarks of
HarperCollins*Publishers* Ltd

First published 2002

10 9 8 7

Mind Maps® is a registered trade mark of The Buzan Group
Original Mind Map concept © Tony Buzan

Plate section illustrations by Alan Burton

A catalogue record for this book
is available from the British Library

ISBN-13   978-0-7225-4049-7
ISBN-10   0-7225-4049-3

Printed and bound in Great Britain by
Martins the Printers Ltd, Berwick upon Tweed

dedication

The Power of Verbal Intelligence is dedicated to my dear Mum, Jean Buzan, who guided me to a love of words and to a deep understanding of their beauty and power; to 'Master Mind Mapper', and phenomenal friend, Vanda North, for her dedication to communicating the message of Mind Mapping; and to Dr Wilfred Funk, whose books on developing word power and his regular column in the *Reader's Digest* inspired me to develop my own Verbal Intelligence.

contents

a word from Barry McGuigan

Youngest ever Irish and British Boxer to be elected to the Boxing Hall of Fame

When I was at the height of my boxing career, it never occurred to me that the knowledge and use of words would become so important to me. At that time, my life was all about rigorous training, dedicated fitness regimes, total discipline and keeping my wits about me in the ring!

After retiring, I started a new and exciting career: that of a commentator for television coverage of boxing. It was then that I realized that my enormous enthusiasm for the sport I was watching needed a much wider range of words and expressions to convey its action and excitement. My every other word being 'terrific' didn't quite do the job. I determined to do something about it.

Inspired by the work of my dear friend Tony Buzan, I began a new path of discovery which has grown into a real passion in my life. I set myself the task of improving my memory and vocabulary and of learning ten new words a week and then applying them, first in conversation, and then in my commentary work. I felt liberated! All the thoughts that I had wanted to convey but which were trapped within me were suddenly there.

I have followed Tony's work for many years, read many of his books and attended his lectures. Tony is to the world of training the mind what the top boxing trainer is to the boxing champion. I still keep to the discipline of learning ten new words each week. I am also determined to help my children have this fundamental ability. We have a game in our house of who can find the most unusual word and I can tell you that I intend to remain the family champion on this one!

Becoming a 'Champion of Words' is possible for anyone: you have Tony and me in your corner, so get out there and grab that title!

acknowledgements

Gratitude and thanks again to my top-of-the-bestseller-lists *Head First* team who have done it once again with *The Power of Verbal Intelligence*! To my Commissioning Editor, Carole Tonkinson; my Editor, Charlotte Ridings; my artist and illustrator, Alan Burton; my designer, Jacqui Caulton; Stephen Bray; Paul Redhead; Toby Watson; Tim Byrne; Yvette Cowles; Jo Lal; and Megan Slyfield. Thank you once again for standing 'on the shoulders of giants' – your own!

Thanks also to my personal team, especially my Publications Manager, Caroline Shott; my External Editor, Vanda North; my Personal Assistant and dear friend, Lesley Bias; and to my dear Mum, Jean Buzan, the best proofreader I have ever met!

fore-word!

your journey to verbal power begins

chapter one

'**"The pen is mightier than the sword"** *only* **if the brain behind it knows how to wield the word!'**

Tony Buzan

what is 'verbal intelligence'?

Verbal Intelligence is the ability to 'juggle' with the alphabet of letters: to combine them into words and sentences. Your Verbal IQ tends to be measured by the size and range of your vocabulary, and by your ability to see relationships between words.

why does verbal intelligence matter?

At the beginning of the 20th century, psychologists observed that there was a direct correlation between vocabulary size and strength, and life-success. In other words, the bigger and better your vocabulary and your Verbal Intelligence, the more successful and confident you will be in your life in general – in your work, in your social and personal life, and in your studies.

Words have tremendous power. Those people who harness the strength of words give themselves the power to persuade, to inspire, to mesmerize, and to influence in all manner of ways the human brain. It is not surprising, then, that words and their power have become one of the most important currencies in the 'Knowledge Revolution' of the 21st century.

how will *the power of verbal intelligence* help me?

The *really* good news is that it is *easy* to improve and expand your verbal skills, and to increase immeasurably your Verbal IQ, and this book will show you how. Barry McGuigan, whom you can read about in Chapter 7, deliberately set about raising his Verbal IQ when he turned to TV commentating after his retirement from the boxing ring, and has since become as adept mentally as he was physically as a fighter.

The Power of Verbal Intelligence is about to take you on one of the most exciting journeys of your life. It is a journey on which you will:

- discover and explore new worlds
- feast your imagination on new concepts and ideas
- learn more about your amazing brain and how to use it
- learn the basic building blocks of word power, enabling you, at a stroke, to expand your current vocabulary by thousands of words
- learn how to use your body to communicate effectively
- rediscover the joy of playing around with words and their meanings
- learn the basic secrets of reading faster and comprehending more
- learn how to mesmerize and entrance others with the power and beauty of your conversation and most importantly, *The Power of Verbal Intelligence* has been designed to make sure that you have fun while you increase your Word Power.

Most importantly, *The Power of Verbal Intelligence* has been designed to make sure that you have fun while you increase your Word Power.

an overview of *the power of verbal intelligence*

The Power of Verbal Intelligence is divided into 10 chapters, each one of which guides you into new areas for improving and expanding your verbal powers.

In this opening chapter I introduce you to the overall structure of the book, so that you can get a clear 'picture' and 'map' of the exciting territory you are about to explore.

You will learn about the history of the development of IQ, and will discover why it is that so many people *think* they are far less intelligent than they really are. The rest of this chapter will be devoted to your first Verbal Workout, in which you will discover new words, play games, be given the first boosts to your Verbal Intelligence and, hopefully, have fun!

Chapter 2: Child's Wordplay – Proof that You are a Natural Verbal Genius

In Chapter 2 I will introduce you to a master of Verbal Intelligence – a total genius in this field who, by example, will show you the secret formulas for improving on all levels your verbal powers.

Who is this paragon of Verbal Intelligence?

The human baby! I will introduce you to the special tools a baby uses to master any language and all verbal situations. A baby learns thousands of new words and hundreds of new verbal skills every year.

Using the same approach, you can do the same.

And, if you think about it, you used to be a baby.

You have already done it once!

With the right help, you can do it again!

Chapter 3: Word Power I – Roots: How to Improve Your Vocabulary, Creativity, Memory and IQ!

Words, like all other structures, are made up of their basic parts. When you know the parts, it is easier to construct the whole. For example, realizing that there are only 26 letters that make up all the words in the English language, makes spelling and word recognition considerably easier than if you had thousands of different letters to learn!

It is exactly the same with word parts – their 'Roots', 'Prefixes' and 'Suffixes'.

In this chapter I will introduce you to 25 key Roots.

As there are only 25 to learn and remember, the task will be a very easy one. It will also be *immensely* rewarding, for each Root is like a magic key, which will open up meaning to many tens and often hundreds of new words.

With these keys in your possession, you will be well on your way to the mastery of the English language.

Chapter 4: Word Power II – Prefixes and Suffixes

Chapter 4 is very similar to Chapter 3, concentrating on those common basic building blocks to words, the beginnings and ends:

Prefixes and Suffixes.

Using the same approach as you used for Roots, you will once again massively multiply the number of words at your command.

Chapter 5: Brain Word – Using Your Brain Power to Develop Your Word Power

How do the following vitally important aspects of your own brain and its functioning relate to the development of your Verbal Intelligence:

- Your memory while it is taking in information?
- Your memory after it has taken in information?
- The right and left brain?
- Study techniques?
- Mind Maps?
- The multi-ordinate meaning of words?

Read this chapter and find out!

Chapter 6: Body Talk – Body Language and How to Improve It

Your Verbal Intelligence has a giant servant – a 'silent helper' – who has phenomenal powers to increase the already phenomenal power of your words.

Your body!

In this chapter I will introduce you to the huge part your body can play in your Verbal Intelligence. You will discover how the way in which you think affects both your body and the way your language is used with your body.

I will also introduce you to that magical musical instrument – your voice – showing you how to 'play' it in ways that will increase your Verbal Intelligence as well as your confidence and popularity.

Chapter 7: Present Yourself – How to Become a Successful Speaker

One of the greatest fears we humans have is that of being seen as a boring conversationalist and a dull speaker. One of our greatest dreams is the opposite: to be a fascinating, witty and enthralling conversationalist, and a mesmerizing presenter.

Happily the fear is unfounded and the dream attainable. In this chapter I will show you how to speak and express yourself with confidence and in a manner that will make you more respected and popular.

Chapter 8: Read On! How to Improve Your Speed, Comprehension and Recall

One of the best indicators of a high Verbal IQ is the ability to read a wide range of materials at a faster speed than average and with greater comprehension.

There are simple ways of achieving these skill levels.

In this chapter I will introduce you to them, showing you how to get a quick grasp of the overall meaning of what you are reading, giving you easy-to-learn-techniques for accelerating your speed, and setting you on the path to lifelong learning and development of your Verbal Intelligence.

In this chapter you will also discover the secrets of the 'Magic Eye'.

Chapter 9: Communication Power – Using Your Verbal Intelligence to Gain Control of Your Life

The ability to communicate clearly and powerfully with words is one of the greatest signs of Verbal Intelligence, and one of the greatest guarantees of lifelong success.

In Chapter 9 you will learn how to become a master of communication. You will learn how to link with and understand others, how to use a Mind Map® as a tool for communicating by telephone, letter, etc., and how to give directions that people both understand and are successful in using. You will also discover some of the secrets of animal communication.

In this chapter I will also introduce you to the Self-audit, in which you will learn how to be your own 'Verbal Doctor', guaranteeing you a long and glowingly healthy verbal life!

Chapter 10: Last Words – Using Your Verbal Intelligence to Increase Your Other Multiple Intelligences

By the time you reach this final chapter, you will already possess a Verbal Intelligence that is considerably more powerful than when you started the book, and will have the tools to ensure it continues to grow.

In 'Last Words' I will introduce you to ways in which the power of your newly empowered Verbal Intelligence can strengthen your overall intelligence.

As I will show, you actually have 10, multiple intelligences, of which Verbal Intelligence is just one. Each of these intelligences strengthens and supports the others, and this Multiplier Effect means that your overall effectiveness and intelligence, not to mention success, *can multiply by hundreds of times!*

✻   ✻   ✻

Features

To assist you in all this, each chapter contains a Verbal Workout, to exercise and strengthen your verbal muscles. These workouts will take the form of exercises and games designed to stretch and stimulate your Word Power. In each Workout there will be specific mental muscle-building verbal games:

- Word Puzzles – half of these games consist of four scrambled words, which you have to unscramble into meaningful words. Selected letters from the answer-words, will, when they themselves are unscrambled, form another one- or two-word answer to a clue that you will have been given. The rest of the puzzles are of a type typically given in standard IQ tests. Give yourself a maximum of five minutes for each one. The answers are on pages 209 – 213. If you score more than five out of ten, you will be doing well!

- Verbal Intelligence Tips – after each of the Word Puzzles, I will give you an insight on how to help your brain solve these verbal games more easily and efficiently. These special insights will build up into a complete Verbal Intelligence Brain Kit, which will help you in future with any similar puzzles, as well as in the wider context of taking any thinking or IQ-type tests.
- Word Power Boosters – at the end of each Verbal Workout, you will be introduced to 10 new words, which will add depth and richness to your existing vocabulary. By the time you have finished *The Power of Verbal Intelligence* you will have accumulated 100 such Power Words!

Although these games are fun and enjoyable entertainment, they are also extremely important tools in developing your Verbal Intelligence. It is 'games' like these that form a significant part of standard IQ tests. Improve your ability with these 'practice' games, and you will raise your IQ.

Throughout the book there are also apposite quotes, case studies to give you insights into how your brain works, and examples of the wonderful thought-enhancing tool I invented especially for the purpose of increasing my own memory and intelligence – the Mind Map®.

a brief history of IQ tests

As has already been mentioned, at the beginning of the 20th century, psychologists observed that there was *a correlation between someone's vocabulary size and strength and their success in life*. This naturally gave rise to a desire to define a person's mental strength, and so the first basic intelligence tests were devised.

These tests measured people's powers of vocabulary, their ability to see relationships between words and between numbers, and logical abilities. Average scores were calculated for different age groups. If your score was average for your age, you scored 100; if your score was slightly below average, your score was determined to be between 90 and 100; and if slightly above average, between 100 and 110. Someone whose scores were measured between 120 and 130 was deemed to be of high intelligence, and a score of 140 or more conferred the status of genius.

These tests became properly known as Intelligence Quotient Tests, or IQ Tests. However, there were two problems with them. First, it was assumed that your IQ score could not and would not change. This, we now know, is completely untrue – you can significantly change and improve your standard IQ score.

The second problem lay in the assumption that what the tests were measuring *was* intelligence, and was all there was *to* intelligence.

Because of these beliefs, education systems around the world became predominantly verbal and mathematical, and being intelligent or smart meant, generally, 'having a way with words'!

However, we are now beginning to realize that Verbal Intelligence is but one of 10 different intelligences – along with Creative, Social, Spatial, Numerical, Spiritual, Personal, Sensory, Sexual and Physical – and that each of the intelligences benefits by the development of the nine others. Thus, as you continue to develop your Verbal Intelligence, you will be simultaneously working on the other nine too!

It is time for your first Verbal Workout!

verbal workout

Word Puzzle Number 1

Welcome to your first Verbal Intelligence Word Puzzle. You will be given four scrambled words. Your first Verbal Intelligence task is to rearrange the letters so that they form a meaningful word. When you have discovered what the word is, place it in the space provided. When you have done this, you will notice that between one and four of the letters in each word are highlighted. These letters take you on to the next stage of the puzzle. Underneath the four words you have unscrambled you will find a clue and a number of blank spaces. The clue will guide you to a one- or two-word answer, found by arranging the 'selected' letters from the first phase of the game into a word or words that satisfy the clue.

This is the first of many such games. In each chapter you will find a similar game, played in the same way. Answers to all the games are in the Answer section, pages 209 – 213.

1. giclo   X __ X __ __
2. nafgymi   __ __ X __ X __ __
3. tonij   X __ __ X __
4. goleyu   __ X __ __ X __

Clue: Having a ball – or more! __ __ __ __ __ __ __ __

Verbal Intelligence Tip

- Whenever you have such Verbal Intelligence questions, *always scan the entire question first.*

Why?

First, because scanning gives your brain the 'whole picture', which means that it can grasp the whole territory and therefore feel in control. Second, if you have scanned all the puzzles/questions, they are 'in' your brain. This means that as your *conscious* brain works on one of the puzzles/questions, your *para-conscious* brain (that 99 per cent-plus powerhouse of your brain that works without you consciously having to control it), will be working on the remaining questions. This makes it much easier to find the correct answer when your conscious attention focuses on the next puzzle/question. In the psychological idiom, you are allowing your brain *to incubate* (sit on, as a bird, for the purpose of hatching) your ideas.

You will know in your daily life that often when you 'can't get' a word, if you allow your brain to 'sleep on it' the word will often pop up into your consciousness. Here, you are simply using this natural process to help raise your Verbal Intelligence.

Word Puzzle Number 2

There is a three-letter word in brackets. When you add, successively, the seven-word beginnings to the three-letter word, each one makes a different meaningful word. What is the word in the brackets?

```
L
M
P
GL        ( __ __ __ )
GR
BR
B
```

How Verbally Intelligent Are You ?

Now that you are becoming familiar with your Verbal IQ, how Verbally Intelligent do you think you are, and more importantly, how Verbally Intelligent do you *want* to be?

On a scale of 1 to 10, with 1 being tongue-tied and not at all Verbally Intelligent, and 10 being eloquent, witty and very Verbally Intelligent, how would you rank your Verbal Intelligence *at the present time?*

Now do the same exercise, but this time indicating on your 1 to 10 scale, how Verbally Intelligent you would like to be *when you finish this book.*

When you have completed these two tasks, start working on converting the real into the ideal.

Get Into Crosswords

Crosswords, Scrabble® and other word games such as word searches and code crackers, are all fantastic ways of stimulating and increasing your Verbal Intelligence. More and more magazines of crosswords and word puzzles are published each month, and they are a great way to try your hand at a variety of different word games.

Check Your Work-word Level

Each different profession has its own specialized vocabulary and expressions. Remember that your Verbal Intelligence has a direct correlation with your success at work. The most successful people in their chosen fields have a vocabulary that ranks in the top 10 per cent for that field.

Begin to keep a list of words that is special to your own profession, and make sure that you aim for that top 10 per cent!

One way to get your mind set for this new vocabularian accomplishment is to pretend that you already are in that top 10 per cent. Act out the role, especially using the kind of vocabulary that is used by people who are successful in your field. If you keep persisting, you soon won't have to act the role – you will be living it!

Set Vocabulary Targets for Other Areas of Your Life

Choose two or three other areas of your life, such as hobbies, social activities, your children's interests/studies, etc., and set yourself goals similar to those you set above for your profession. By doing this you will be following the example of a body-builder who trains a wide range of muscles, rather than simply one. You will therefore develop a well-balanced body of vocabulary skills.

Listen for New Words

Listen out for new and unusual words as you go about your daily life – on the TV or radio, at the local shops or a meeting at work. Adding this new focus of attention will not only make you a better vocabularian; it will make you a better listener, and therefore more popular and successful with others. Keep a notepad or some form of recorder always with you so that you can jot down new words of special interest, meaning or beauty. At regular intervals, either at the end of the day or week, transfer your new words to a master list. When you come across such words, try to use them in sentences at least five times in a day – this will help you remember them.

Look for New Words

Do exactly the same with your eyes as you did with your ears, checking
newspapers, magazines, books and screens for new and exciting
words. Transfer them to your lists. When you are doing both these
listening and looking exercises, be on the look-out for words that reflect
or relate to your senses of sight, sound, smell, taste, touch and
movement. This will both improve your vocabulary and widen its
range, making you a better, more confident communicator.

Make a Mind Map

Build a mini Mind Map® on all the advantages an improved vocabulary
and increased Verbal Intelligence will give you. In the centre of page 20
is a little image which summarizes Verbal Intelligence. Branching from
it are 10 main branches, and from each of these, three sub-branches.
Copy the Mind Map® onto a large sheet of paper. On the main
branches print, clearly, the first 10 key ideas that come to your mind
when you think of the ways in which an increased Verbal Intelligence
would improve your life and your chances of success. When you have
completed the first 10 ideas, think of three more ideas that branch
from each of those main 10 and, in the same way, print them neatly on
the lines provided. When you have completed the exercise, place your
Mind Map® somewhere where you will constantly be reminded of just
how valuable an increased Verbal Intelligence is to your entire life.

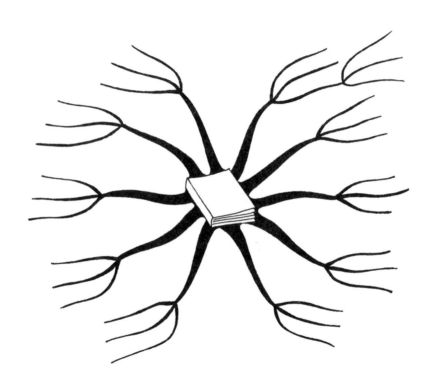

Invest in a Good Dictionary!

Make sure you get a good dictionary. A good dictionary is the ultimate guide and support for anyone wishing to improve their Verbal Intelligence.

Word Power Booster Number 1

As this is your first Word Power Booster, it is *intro*ductory! Below each word are four different definitions. Choose the one you think is closest to the correct meaning. (Answers are on page 213 – 15.)

1 INTRODUCE (in-tro-*jóos*)
- (a) To stick a needle into
- (b) To become a Duke
- (c) To bring in or present
- (d) To do first

2 INTROFLEX (*ín*-tro-flex)
- (a) To bend outward
- (b) To bend inward
- (c) To build muscle
- (d) To look strong

3 INTROCEPTIVE (in-tro-*sép*-tif)
- (a) Capable of receiving into itself
- (b) The beginning of a reception
- (c) A method of preparing food
- (d) Able to perceive the inside of things

---

4 INTROGRESSION (in-tro-gré-shon)

   (a) The act of going in; entering
   (b) Falling behind
   (c) Thinking about things
   (d) Becoming aggressive

5 INTROJECT (in-tro-jékt)

   (a) To inject
   (b) To ask
   (c) To discard
   (d) To throw into

6 INTROMIT (in-tro-mít)

   (a) To lay on hands
   (b) To stop
   (c) To allow to enter; insert
   (d) To jump across

7 INTROSPECT (in-tro-spékt)

   (a) To look for glasses
   (b) To inspect
   (c) To look outward
   (d) To look within

8 INTROMISSION (in-tro-*mí*-shon)

    (a)   To start a break

    (b)   To insert

    (c)   The beginning of a project

    (d)   To start religious conversion

9 INTROVERT (in-tro-*vért*) (noun)

    (a)   One who turns inward

    (b)   Something upside down

    (c)   Dressed in green

    (d)   One who stands vertically; good poise

10 INTROPRESSION (in-tro-*pré*-shon)

    (a)   To introduce the media

    (b)   Pressure within

    (c)   To make heavy

    (d)   To press upon

chapter two

'Language is the immediate gift of God.'

Noah Webster

In this chapter I will introduce you to the best language learner the world has ever known – that master of Verbal Intelligence, the human baby!

I will show you the 'secret' formulas that babies use to achieve their astounding results. As a consequence, you will discover new approaches to: 'cheating'/copying; play as a learning tool; the making of mistakes and 'failure'; creating success from 'disaster'; general attitudes to learning; and the incredible 'genius power' of Persistence.

You will come to realize that, as a baby, you used all the right tools to develop your Verbal Intelligence. As your life progressed, you discarded them, and as a result the development of your Verbal Intelligence came to a grinding halt.

However, all you have to do now is pick these tools up again and continue with your verbal growth. This time around, you'll not only have the tools you once used to learn and remember thousands of new words – you will have the additional tools from *The Power of Verbal Intelligence,* which will enable you to use the 'baby skills' as a launching pad for your own accelerated development!

You will end up as an even better vocabulary and language learner than the baby.

Let's start with the fascinating story of a Japanese musician, Suzuki, who made some amazing discoveries about your incredible Verbal Intelligence potential.

Suzuki's Story

Suzuki was a Japanese teacher, musician and instrument maker. He had two special paradigm-shifts in his awareness that changed his life forever, and which are at this very moment changing the lives of millions and the way the world thinks about all babies and their Verbal and Creative Intelligences.

Suzuki's first revelation came when he was visiting a giant incubarium for Japanese larks.

The Japanese breeders of these songbirds take literally thousands of eggs and incubate them in giant, warm, silent halls that act as a gigantic nest. Silent, that is, with the exception of one

---

sound – that of a lark Master Singer, a veritable song-bird Beethoven!

Suzuki noticed to his amazement that *every* little chick that hatched, automatically began to copy the master singer. After a few days he observed that each chick, having started out by purely copying songs, began to develop its own variations on the original Master Song. The breeders waited until the chick musicians had developed their own styles, and then selected from them the next Master Singer, and so the process developed.

'Astounding!' thought Suzuki. 'If a bird's tiny, tiny brain can learn so perfectly, then surely the human brain, with its vastly superior abilities, should be able to do the same and *better!*'

This line of reasoning led Suzuki to his next revelation, which, when he announced it, made many of his friends think that he had lost a large number of his own brain cells.

Suzuki, in a delirium of enthusiasm for what he had realized, rushed around telling everyone he knew of his remarkable discovery: that every Japanese child learns to speak Japanese!

His friends and colleagues patted him on the shoulder, informing him rather firmly they were actually already aware of that. 'But No! No!' declared Suzuki, 'they really *do*, and it's amazing!'

Suzuki was correct. Like Newton before him, he had discovered something that was so obvious no one could see it – that *any* baby, born in *any* country, automatically learns, within two years, the language of that country.

This means that *every* normal baby's brain is capable of learning millions of potential languages.

If you, dear reader, had been born in and lived for the first few years of your life in a totally different country from that you are familiar with now, your own baby brain would have absorbed that language as rapidly and fluently as you now speak your own main tongue.

If you, for example, were a Caucasian baby and had been born in Beijing, you would not have looked up with your little baby eyes and thought 'Oh, Chinese. Far too complex for me! Think I'll stay silent for the rest of my life!'

Not only would you have learned the language of that country, you would have learned the specific language sounds of the special area of that country in which you had been born – your accent.

What Suzuki had discovered was that the voice/ear/brain system was a virtually perfect copying machine, with an almost infinite capacity to learn the music (words and rhythms) of an infinite number of languages.

What's more, it didn't matter whether the language was Chinese, Portuguese, Music-ese, Maths-ese, Art-ese, Burmese, or Japanese. So long as a baby was given the right learning environment and proper encouragement, it could learn *anything!*

mimicking

What Suzuki had discovered was the Brain Principle of Mimicking. This principle states that your brain is designed to learn by copying the best

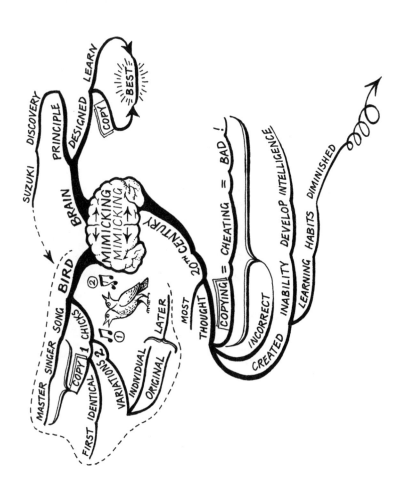

child's wordplay –
proof that you are a natural verbal genius

of what it sees around it. If it is allowed to do this, it will be capable of ongoing learning at an accelerated rate.

For the bulk of the 20th century we incorrectly thought of mimicking as copying, copying as cheating, and cheating as bad. With this incorrect way of thinking, we created habits of learning that increasingly diminished our abilities to develop our intelligences, especially Verbal Intelligence.

We even came up with ridiculous assumptions to back-up this incorrect thinking, such as that once you are past the age of 10, the development of Verbal Intelligence becomes much more difficult, and that once you are past the age of 25 it becomes virtually impossible.

Nothing could be further from the truth.

By applying the principle of mimicking, as the songbird chicks do, and the additional knowledge you will gain from *The Power of Verbal Intelligence*, you will be able to increase your rate of vocabulary acquisition and word power at a pace that makes a baby's seem embarrassingly slow by comparison!

play

When the baby is 'at work' dealing with the massive tasks of survival and learning, its main tool is Play.

Play is the method the universe has designed for allowing the brain to learn most easily.

How is this so?

Because play involves activity that is enjoyable, often amusing, and always imaginative. It usually involves physical activity, often vigorous and long, and demands that the brain makes new associations between things.

You will know that all babies love to play, especially with words. They roll them around in their mouths, often purposely mispronounce them to make them more interesting or funny, play with different variations and combinations of words and parts of words, change the pitch, speed, tone and volume of their voices, and are *always* curious about new words and their meanings and associations.

Unfortunately during the last two centuries learning has been made much more serious, and the element of play removed except in the classrooms of superb teachers. Even at the beginning of the 21st century this is still happening. In America some educators are leading a movement to eliminate play from schools altogether, including playtime. Their argument? That if you eliminate play and playtime, you will save time and get far better results from the young brains because they will be 100 per cent dedicated to 'serious' work. Such a policy is like saying that if we remove children's legs their bodies would be lighter and therefore more mobile!

It is by applying the Brain Principle of Play that babies and children rapidly develop their Verbal Intelligence.

You can begin to see the implications for yourself ...

love of learning

Another of the baby's secret weapons in the development of its Verbal Intelligence is its boundless love of learning. This love is both led and fed by an insatiable curiosity.

The instant the baby's brain asks the next question or wants to know the 'next step', all its senses open, and all its energies are immediately directed to the achievement of that answer; that goal.

This openness and focus are exactly what the brain needs to take in, understand and remember new verbal information.

'The use of increasingly complex and sophisticated language structures, and the units (vocabulary) which make up those structures, is one of the defining characteristics of evolutionary advance and development. The training and nurturing of your skill in this area is your natural right, your own responsibility, and a rare opportunity. If you grasp it, it will provide you with exceptional benefits. Claim it. Accept it. Develop it!'

Tony Buzan

Ironically the baby's love of learning is accompanied by something that most adults think is not acceptable or permissible, but which forms the foundation-stone in the development of Verbal Intelligence. It is the next 'Baby Secret'.

making mistakes / 'failing'

Does the baby make mistakes?

Yes!

More than the average adult learner?

Many more!

How can it be that a super-learner like the baby makes more mistakes than the average adult, who does not learn so fast?

Because the baby knows the secret: *making mistakes and experiencing 'failures' is one of the fastest ways to accelerate your learning.*

If you don't make mistakes it means that you have not tried. If you do not try you will never learn.

The baby has hit upon the secret that if you combine your love of learning with creativity and taking risks, *you will not only make more mistakes than most other people, you will have many more successes.*

All research shows that the world's great geniuses simply carried on using this Baby Success Formula. They wrote millions of words, painted millions of brush strokes, composed millions of notes, and formulated millions of ideas. They then discarded much of it, and kept the best!

'Language is the dress of thought.'

Samuel Johnson

There is one other secret principle at which the baby is a world champion:

persistence

Combined with the love of learning and the making of mistakes, the baby realizes that without persistence, no progress is ever made.

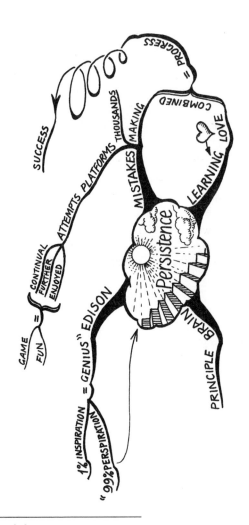

Just think of how many times a baby sometimes tries to pronounce a complex word before getting it finally right; it is sometimes *hundreds* of 'failures'.

Does the baby go into a sulk and think something like 'What's the point?! I've tried thousands of times and still can't get this bloody word! This language-learning lark is too hard; it's not for me – I give up!'

Of course not.

The baby uses each mistake as a platform for the next attempt. While doing this it makes a game of the whole thing, relishing the process, and always keeping its eye on the inevitable success of the goal.

'Language is the armoury of the human mind.'

Coleridge

You are now ready to enter the playground!

verbal workout

Word Puzzle Number 3

tustea	_ _ _ _ X X
lapcita	_ _ _ _ X _ X
lacyrit	_ _ X X _ _ _
hubog	_ _ _ X X

Clue: Makes you happy and fit _ _ _ _ _ _ _ _

Verbal Intelligence Tip

■ Always answer the easiest questions first, no matter where they are in the list or linear order you have in front of you.

Why?

Because answering the easiest questions first will allow you to 'get one under your belt', your para-conscious brain will realize that there is already less to do than when you started, and this will significantly reduce stress, while simultaneously boosting your confidence.

Secondly, answering these questions first will establish a habit in your brain – the habit of *success*. And success breeds success!

Word Puzzle Number 4

Insert the word that completes the first word and begins the second.

(Clue: finish)

T R (__ __ __) I V E

Mimic the Best

In exactly the same way that a baby copies those people it considers to be the most powerful and successful (its parents!), copy those experts, public figures, actors, sports personalities or people from your own profession whom you consider to be 'Top of the Pops' in the imaginative use of words, as well as in range and clarity.

Make a point of observing and studying them, noting especially interesting words that they use, as well as their methods of delivery.

Play with Words

Remember that one of the baby's most powerful learning tools is 'play'. Apply this to the development of your own vocabulary. Mix sections of different words to come up with startling new words and meanings, and enjoy the freedom this gives you. Make up doggerel verse, rhymes and palindromes (phrases that read the same both forwards and backwards – 'Madam, I'm Adam' for example!).

Shakespeare, one of the highest Verbal Intelligences the planet has ever known, loved to play with words, and as a result added over 200 new words and expressions that are now common to the global language. Try to catch up with him!

It was this freedom of mind and ability to create that gave rise to the study of Holanthropy, the discipline that arose from my own frustration at not being able to find any discipline in which I could study the whole (Greek 'holos') human-being (Greek 'anthropos').

Another new word you might enjoy comes from a friend of mine and a teacher of Holanthropy, Lex McKee. A lover of words as well as a musician and artist, Lex had been very happy with the word onomatopoeic (a word whose sound imitates that of the noise or action it describes, such as 'buzz').

However, he suddenly realized that this word applied only to sound, and as he was also an artist, he wanted a word that appealed also to the sense of vision. He simply took 'onomatopoeic', and pasted on to it a preliminary 'v', thus creating 'vonomatopoeic' – a word meaning 'sounding and *looking* like the thing described!

Alphabet fridge magnets are the perfect fun way to explore and make up new words and meanings. What's more, the entire family can join in, creating more and more words on that wonderful public notice and message board that is many people's fridge door!

Look Out for Unknown Words!

Keep a constant look out for words of which you don't know the meaning, and also for words that are completely new.

For many adults, facing the fact that they 'don't know' is disturbing. As a result they tend to try to avoid such situations. If you look at this 'formula for behaviour' for a moment, you will realize that it is a formula for disaster! If you only stay safely in areas that are completely known to you, and always avoid those that are not, what will you ever learn?

Nothing!

The baby is exactly the opposite. Why? Because a baby loves not knowing! Not knowing opens up the infinite opportunity for learning fresh, new and exciting things. The baby is purely ignorant, and ignorant (which comes from the Latin '*ignorare*') simply means 'to not know'. Realize that the more you know you know, the more you will know that there is still more to know!

Approach your pursuit of new and fresh knowledge like a baby does – with enthusiasm and gusto!

Give Your Brain a Healthy Diet

Your brain survives on the four foods of *Information, Nutrition, Oxygen* and *Love*. One of your brain's main sources of information is *Vocabulary* and *Language*. Therefore feed your brain a healthy diet of words, making sure that you 'eat' regularly, that your 'diet' is varied, that you constantly supply yourself with 'fresh food' and that you never 'fast' for too long. Sometimes it's good to binge!

Learn From Your Mistakes

As with ignorance, many adults also are discomforted by and afraid of making mistakes, especially with words. They, mistakenly, think that this shows them to be slow, unintelligent and somehow not worthy.

Nothing could be further from the truth!

If you want to learn how to speak any vocabulary brilliantly, learn from the greatest language learners there are – babies and children. They seldom hide in the safety of words they know; their preference is to leap for the stars, and to make as many mistakes as are necessary to get there.

That is why they often prefer hard or 'more difficult' words: these give them a better game to play in acquiring them, and often lead to mistakes that are much more humorous and which provide many more belly laughs than the 'correct' ones!

We now know that mistakes are not an *impediment* to learning; mistakes are the *golden pathway* to learning.

Enjoy all of yours from now on ...

Become Friends with Words

You bring your feelings and emotions more into play when you increase your Verbal Intelligence. Many people mistakenly think of words as 'intelligent', 'analytical', 'hard' and 'cold'. And who would really want to have a relationship with anything (or anyone) that only had those qualities?

But words are in fact 'wondrous', 'imaginative', 'sensual', 'sexy', 'warm', 'delicious' and many other things which would make you lust after a relationship with anything or anyone possessing these qualities.

As soon as you start making friends with words, as babies do, they make friends with you, and allow you to meet, learn from and play with them much more rapidly and with thousands of times greater enjoyment and fun than before.

Persist in Your Pursuit of Verbal Power

Remember that one of the prime qualities used to describe the incredible intelligence and accomplishments both of babies and the great geniuses is that single word: *persistence*. The *Oxford English Dictionary* defines 'persistence' as meaning: 'To continue firmly in an opinion or course of action in spite of difficulty or opposition; to continue to persist.' It comes from the Latin *'per'* and *'sistere'* – 'to stand firm'.

If you steadfastly *pursue* your goal of Verbal Intelligence, you will *become* much more Verbally Intelligent, and will approach the incredible skills of the baby and the genius in this area. Persist and you will overcome all obstacles to learning. Persist and your mistakes will turn into successes. Persist and you will acquire thousands of new word-friends.

Persist!

Word Power Booster Number 2

In this vocabulary booster section I introduce you to some fascinating adjectives. They will spice up your conversation, adding richness and depth to it. Choose the definition that you think is closest to the correct meaning from the four options given for each. (Answers on page 215 – 16.)

1 DIDACTIC (dy-*dák*-tik)

- (a) Teacher-like; instructive
- (b) Aggressive
- (c) Explosive
- (d) Like an extinct bird

2 SURREPTITIOUS (surep-*tísh*-us)

- (a) Grey in colour
- (b) Serrated
- (c) Stealthy or secret
- (d) Completely silent

3 HERETICAL (heh-*rét*-ikal)

- (a) Deserving of punishment
- (b) At the present time
- (c) Greek behaviour
- (d) Revolutionary; contrary to the official/established viewpoint

4 COPIOUS (*kópe*-eus)

- (a) Able
- (b) Abundant; plentiful
- (c) Religious
- (d) Relating to the police

5 IMPERATIVE (im-*pé*-rra-tif)
- (a) Royal
- (b) Relating to the empire
- (c) Vital
- (d) Strong

6 INEFFACEABLE (in-e-*fáce*-abul)
- (a) To confront
- (b) Incapable of being erased; indelible
- (c) Female face
- (d) Building

7 INESTIMABLE (in-*ést*-im-abul)
- (a) Not enough time
- (b) Priceless; immeasurable
- (c) Unfriendly
- (d) Timetable

8 UNPRECEDENTED (un-*préss*-e-den-ted)
- (a) Never known or done before
- (b) Description of dental procedures
- (c) Damaged
- (d) Before production

9 UNEQUIVOCAL (un-e-*kwívo*-cal)

- (a) Different voices
- (b) Unambiguous; leaving no doubt
- (c) Unequal
- (d) Discordant choir

10 CATEGORICAL (kata-*górr*-ical)

- (a) Bluntly and unconditionally expressed
- (b) Dividing into categories
- (c) About cats
- (d) Vaguely defined

chapter three

'Words are the instruments that make thought possible.'

Judd

'Words are the body of thought.'

· Carlyle

In this chapter and the next you are going to learn more about the incredible power of words.

I will guide you through recent history, showing you how words developed as a 'secret power', and will introduce you to research that show why this was so.

---

word power I – roots: how to improve your vocabulary, creativity, memory and IQ!

The bulk of this chapter and the next are then devoted to a veritable feast of building blocks of vocabulary and Verbal Intelligence: *Roots, Prefixes* and *Suffixes*.

With the mastery of these your Verbal Intelligence will inevitably improve, and your life will change irrevocably!

Case Study – A Word About Business

In America, Dr Johnson O'Connor, who worked at the Human Engineering Laboratory in Boston, was fascinated by the relationship of vocabulary and professional success. He gave a vocabulary test to 100 young men who were studying to be industrial executives. Five years after the original experiment, Dr O'Connor checked how successful the young businessmen had been in their careers.

The correlation was astonishing. Of those who had scores in the top 25 per cent of the original vocabulary test, *all were in executive positions*.

Of those who had scores in the lowest 25 per cent of the original test, not a single one had become an executive!

---

words and power

Since the dawn of civilization, words have had an aura of mystery, magic and power to them. The earliest form of writing (Cuneiform) developed in the Near East, in Mesopotamia, to allow rulers to keep accurate records of what taxes were due and who had paid them, and for other bureaucratic records, such as details of amounts of grain stored and distributed.

In ancient Egypt the priests were the 'keepers of the word'. They tried to keep the art of writing and reading secret, because doing so gave them tremendous power to manipulate both knowledge and people. For the next four thousand years leaders in all societies kept this special power to themselves, communicating in the secret codes of higher vocabulary and writing, while the ignorant masses around reacted with awe, superstition and fear at the power that words held over them.

'We rule men with words.'

(Napoleon)

This power was the power over knowledge; the power of persuasion; the power to inspire; the power to mesmerize; and the power to control and lead. In other words, it was the power to affect the human brain.

---

word power I – roots: how to improve your
vocabulary, creativity, memory and IQ!

49

Two of our modern words, which you would never have thought would have derived from this history, do – **'spell'** and **'glamour'**!

As recently as the great European Renaissance, the time of Queen Elizabeth I and the master-works of Shakespeare, still surprisingly few people could read or write. The record books show that most of the young people who had to sign for a marriage licence did so not with their name, but with a cross.

The ability to read and write was looked upon by the ordinary people with awe, and those who were able to do so were often considered to be dabbling in some form of magic. Those who could write could, in general, spell.

So the logic in the ignorant and fearful mind was that those who could spell possessed a magic that could mysteriously and ominously control others. As a word could be considered a 'spell' the owner of such esoteric knowledge, by using words, was 'casting spells': QED!

The word 'glamour' has a similarly interesting etymology, or derivation.

In the 17th century the language of the intellectuals was predominantly Latin. In this they used to write, converse and increase their grip on social, economic and political power.

To 'tie their words together' they used the mystical concept of 'grammar'. Grammar became an idea that linked with those who had authority and power. As time passed the first 'R' in grammar slowly mutated, as 'R's often do over time, to the letter 'L'. Thus 'grammar' eventually became 'glamour', a word that is still applied to those who emanate an aura of power, elegance and control.

Words still hold a spell over us, and rightly so. As you continue to improve your Verbal Intelligence, you will increasingly become a Word Magician.

word roots

One of the best ways to become an adept verbal magician is to study the Roots of the words we commonly use.

When you study word Roots, not only do you instantly increase the power of your vocabulary and Verbal Intelligence, you come to realize an important fact: words are not cold, abstract, dead things. They are warm, emotional, meaningful and very much alive.

Like all living things words are conceived, born and grow to maturity. Eventually they pass on their meaning and energy to new word forms and languages.

The study of Roots is the study of fascinating stories about the creation and birth of words. You are now involved in this wonderful study, and therefore can be called an 'etymologist'. The word 'etymology', can be traced back to the Greek '*etymon*' (meaning 'true or original meaning') and also to the Greek '*-logia*', 'study of', which, in turn, comes from the Greek '*logos*', meaning 'word'!

So you can now truthfully say that you are an etymologist: one who is interested in and studies the science of true or original meanings.

---

word power I – roots: how to improve your
vocabulary, creativity, memory and IQ!

51

Each Root is like a little being in suspended animation. By studying it you bring it to life, allowing the beautiful imagery, history and poetry that is the word's essence to live again. For example, if you listen to classical music you will often hear that a piece is entitled 'Opus 1' or 'Opus 104'. People often think that this means something like 'creative inspiration' or 'musical masterpiece', but what does it *actually* mean?

If you know your Roots you will know the answer. The Latin meaning of this Root is simply 'work'. Knowing this you get an instantaneous insight into the true working of the creative mind. All the magnificent music you hear is not the result of 'airy fairy' artists. It is the result of years of dedicated and passionate study and *work*.

Roots, then, are like the centres of mini Mind Maps®, which radiate out into all sorts of wonderful branches, associations and ramifications. They are little universes in themselves that illuminate the dark skies of verbal ignorance.

You are about to enter the worlds of the Romans and the Greeks, to explore 25 such universes.

Root Number 1

arch

Meaning: ruler (from the Greek '*archos*')

'This root will help you become the **architect** of your own linguistic future, and will help you to rise in the **hierarchy** of vocabularians!'

Example words

- Matri**arch** noun. The female head of a family or tribe.
  'She ruled her entire family with a kind heart coupled with an iron will – she was a real **matriarch!**'
- Patri**arch** noun. The male head of a family.
  'The Oscar-winning film *The Godfather* was about an ultimate **patriarch** – the Don of an Italian Mafia family.'
- Olig**arch**y noun. A small group of people who rule or govern a state.
  'The great Greek philosopher Plato thought that an enlightened **oligarchy** of "Philosopher Kings" was a better form of rule than allowing matters of state to be run by the relatively ignorant populace.'

Root Number 2

claim   clam

Meaning: to declare; call; carry out (from the Latin '*clamare*')
  'With this root you will be able to **claim** additional verbal territory, and to further increase the probability that your increasing verbal skills and performances will be met with **acclaim!**'

word power I – roots: how to improve your vocabulary, creativity, memory and IQ!

53

Example words

- **Declaim** verb. To make a formal speech.
  'I wish to **declaim** on the subject of Holanthropy.'
- **Proclaim** verb. To make known to the public.
  'Our new knowledge about the brain and its ability to learn is so important that we must all take every opportunity available to us to **proclaim** it globally.'
- **Exclaim** verb. To cry out suddenly, as in surprise.
  'When she first saw all her friends gathered for her surprise party, it made her **exclaim** in a manner that brought a smile to everyone's face.'

Root Number 3

corp   corpor

Meaning: body (from the Latin '*corpus*')

'The **incorporation** of this root into your vocabulary will hearten the other roots and will create among them an **esprit de corps!**'

Example words

- **Corps** noun. A group of people organized into the single body for a common service.
  'Many young people join the Peace **Corps** in order to help other people around the world, and to widen their knowledge and experience of the planet.'

- In**corpor**ate verb. To form into a body of persons by legal enactment.
  'They decided to **incorporate** themselves into a company, in order to maximize the rewards they could reap from their clever idea.'
- **Corpor**eal adjective. Having a material body.
  'It is important to both distinguish and integrate matters **corporeal**, intellectual and spiritual.'

Root Number 4

dic   dict

Meaning: to say or declare (from the Latin '*dictare*')
  'This root will act as an **indicator** to where it itself appears!'

Example words

- **Dict**ionary noun. A reference book of what words 'say'.
  'A **dictionary** is a very useful tool to have when you are developing your Verbal Intelligence.'
- Pre**dict**ion noun. A declaration of what will happen in the future.
  'It is my confident **prediction** that more and more people will become interested in developing their Multiple Intelligences.'
- **Dict**ion noun. The correct choice or use of words.
  'He spoke clearly and beautifully – his **diction** was close to perfect.'

---

word power I – roots: how to improve your
vocabulary, creativity, memory and IQ!

55

Root Number 5

fac   fact

Meaning: to make (from the Latin *'facere'*, *'factus'*, to create or construct)

'When you have finished this exercise you will have a greater **facility** with any word containing these two roots, and from it you will derive great **satisfaction**!'

Example words

- Satis**fac**tion noun. The state in which everything is made right.
  'I can't get no **satisfaction**!'
- **Fac**ile adjective. Easily achieved.
  'It was a **facile** victory, in which he check-mated his opponent with no apparent effort.'
- **Fac**totum noun. One who can do many things
  'The irreplaceable employee was a **factotum**; she did everything.'

Root Number 6

fic   fect

Meaning: to make (from the Latin *'fictus'*, to form or fashion)

'With this root you will be the beneficiary of that which will make you far more **proficient** with your vocabulary, and will help you on your road to verbal **perfection**!'

Example words

- Magnificent adjective. Made grandly.
  'The Taj Mahal is a **magnificent** example of architecture at its best.'
- Deification noun. Making a god out of something or worshipping something as a god.
  'The **deification** of the sun and moon were a major part of most cultures' spiritual development.'
- Efficacious adjective. Effective; producing the desired effect.
  'It was a risky experiment, with happily **efficacious** results.'

Root Number 7

gnosi   cognosc

Meaning: to know (from the Latin '*noscere*' and '*cognoscere*')
    'This root will help you **recognize** an entirely new range of words, none of which, to you, will be able to remain completely **incognito**!'

Example words

- **Cognis**ant adjective. Being aware; knowing.
  'When you have finished reading *The Power of Verbal Intelligence* you will be **cognisant** of a whole new universe of words and meaning.'
- Pro**gnosi**s noun. A forecast; foretelling the course of events.

word power I – roots: how to improve your
vocabulary, creativity, memory and IQ!

57

'With its new understanding of its own brain and potential, the **prognosis** for the future of the human race is looking increasingly bright.'

- Cognoscente noun. A connoisseur; a person who is 'in the know'.
'The gathering of top chefs represented one of the greatest gatherings of **cognoscente** the food world had ever known.'

Root Number 8

intellect intellig

Meaning: the power to know and think (from the Latin '*inter*', between, and '*legere*', to choose)

'This clever root will help you increase your **intelligibility** when communicating, and will have others impressed by your towering **intellect**!'

Example words

- **Intellect**ual noun. One with knowledge who knows how to reason and understand objectively.
'Because of her vast learning, she was considered one of the university's top **intellectual** brains.
- **Intellig**ible adjective. Can be easily understood.
'Despite the complexity of the subject, her clear explanation made it completely **intelligible** to her audience.'

- **Intellig**encia noun. The intellectual, artistic, musical and thinking class of people in society.
  'Plato thought that it was from the **intelligencia** that the rulers of the state or nation should be chosen.'

Root Number 9

liber

Meaning: free (from the Latin '*liber*', '*libertas*')
  'This root will open many new words to you and will help **liberate** your mind!'

Example words

- **Liber**alize verb. To make more free.
  'Poets, painters and philosophers have, throughout history, attempted to **liberalize** minds from ignorance.'
- **Liberalism** noun. The belief that one should be respectful and accepting of behaviour or opinions different from one's own; open to new ideas.
  'Democracy and **liberalism** are often seen to go hand-in-hand.'
- **Liber**tarianism noun. An extremely **laissez faire** political philosophy advocating only minimal state intervention in the lives of citizens.
  '**Libertarianism** is at the other end of the political spectrum from totalitarianism.'

word power I – roots: how to improve your vocabulary, creativity, memory and IQ!

59

Root Number 10

logo   log

Meaning: 'word' (from the Greek '*logos*')

'This root will certainly help you to become more **logical** in your thinking, and hopefully will encourage you to become a **logodidalist**.'

Example words

- **Logo**latary noun. The worship of logic.
  'Her love of the Greek philosophers and their introduction of logic into the thought systems of the world led her increasingly towards **logolatary**.'
- **Logo**gog noun. One who legislates on word meanings'.
  'The publishers of the new dictionary hired the nation's top **logogog** to guarantee the quality of their product.'
- '**Logo**daedaly noun. Playing cleverly and wittily with words; a verbal juggler.
  'With his newly enriched vocabulary he began to entertain his friends with **logodaedaly**.'

Root Number 11

magna   magni

Meaning: great (from the Latin '*magnus*')

'This great root will help you to increase the **magnitude** of your already large vocabulary, and to realize the power, beauty and **magnificence** of the language you speak.'

Example words

- **Magni**fy verb. To make greater.
  'Both telescopes and microscopes **magnify** the macro-cosmos and the micro-cosmos, making them more readily comprehendible to our inquisitive minds.'
- **Magna**te noun. Someone of great wealth and power.
  'When the shipping **magnate** visited the city, he arranged a meeting with those wielding similar power.'
- **Magna**nimous adjective. Great-hearted; generous.
  'He was **magnanimous** to the point of becoming a saint.'

Root Number 12

mem

Meaning: remember (from the Latin '*memor*', mindful)
  'This root will quite obviously help improve your **memory** by enabling you more easily to understand and **remember** words, which, when you use them, will make you more **memorable** to others!'

word power I – roots: how to improve your vocabulary, creativity, memory and IQ!

61

Example words

- **Mem**oir noun. A record of things you wish to remember.
  'He thought his life had been so exciting and original that he
  decided to write a **memoir** of it in the form of an autobiography.
- **Mem**orabilia noun. Things judged worthy of keeping for purposes
  of memory.
  'Many people's attics or basements are filled with **memorabilia** that
  help them to recall the special people, places and events in their
  lives.'
- Im**mem**orial adjective. Long past; having occurred so long ago that
  there is no record of it.
  'Human beings have composed poetry and songs from time
  immemorial.'

Root Number 13

neo

Meaning: new or recent (from the Greek '*neos*')
  'At this stage in your vocabulary development you will no longer be a
neophyte; you will have become a skilled user of words and language,
and will have given great pleasure and stimulation to your **neocortex**!'

Example words

- **Neo**phyte noun. A novice, a beginner, a new convert.

'As he was a **neophyte** in the spiritual order, he decided to listen first and speak second.'

- **Neo**lithic adjective. The 'new' era when humans began to grow crops and domesticate animals.
  'The **Neolithic** era marked one of the great creative leaps in the development of humankind's thinking.'
- **Neo**logy noun. The use of new words in a language.
  '**Neology** has traditionally added to the richness and variety of the spoken and written language.'

Root Number 14

nov

Meaning: new (from the Latin '*nova*', '*novus*')
'This root will help you become more **innovative**, allowing you to think in **novel** ways. It might even inspire you to **renovate** areas of your life and even to write a **novel**!'

Example words

- **Nov**elist noun. One who writes a new literary work.
  'After many years of factual writing, the author decided to use his imagination to write a major new work of fiction; he decided to become a **novelist**.'

- **Nov**ice noun. One who is new at any skill or enterprise.

---

word power I – roots: how to improve your vocabulary, creativity, memory and IQ!

63

'Although he was a **novice** at soccer, his footballing skills were those of a seasoned campaigner.'

- Super**nov**a noun. A star which suddenly explodes, taking on a new form. In the process it shines with millions of times its usual brightness.

  'The crab nebula is a giant cloud-like structure which is the gigantic remains of a star that became a **supernova** many millions of years ago.'

Root Number 15

nunci nounc

Meaning: speak; declare; announce (from the Latin verb '*nuntiare*')

'With this root you will be able to **announce** that your **enunciation** and ability to **pronounce** have improved!'

Example words

- Pro**nunci**ation noun. The sound of the utterance; the articulation of the spoken word.

  'It is interesting that many people incorrectly pronounce "**pronunciation**" "**pronounciation**"!'

- E**nunci**ate verb. To pronounce carefully and accurately.

  'In order to make himself easily understood, he decided to use simple language and to **enunciate** clearly.'

Root Number 16

opus   oper

Meaning: work (from the Latin 'opus')

'With this root, which has also come to describe a large piece of choral music, you will better understand the nature of **co-operation**, will derive added appreciation from the "little **oper**as" known as **operettas**, and hopefully will become an even smarter **operator**!'

Example words

- **Oper**ative adjective. Causing to operate; having the power to act. 'The machine, after months of not working, suddenly and mysteriously became **operative**.'
- **Oper**alogue noun. A declamation on an opera, which presents a summary of the story.
  'Before going to see *Madame Butterfly*, they were pleased to be able to attend an **operalogue** given by the conductor.'
- **Opus** noun. A musical work or composition.
  'Baron Philippe Rothschilde and Robert Mondavi, the great French and American winemakers, decided to call the first wine they made together "**Opus** I".'

word power I – roots: how to improve your vocabulary, creativity, memory and IQ!

65

Root Number 17

pan

Meaning: all (from the Greek '*pan*')

'This word should be housed in your **pantheon** of great roots, for it will help you on your road to **pansophy** or universal wisdom!'

Example words

- **Pan**theism noun. The belief that identifies God with the Universe, or regards the Universe as a manifestation of God.
  'She regarded the forces of nature as divine, she was a **pantheist**.'
- **Pan**acea noun. A cure for all ills.
  'Many people believe that love is the ultimate **panacea**.'
- **Pan**demic adjective. Something that is widespread.
  'The great flu **pandemic** spread across all of Europe.'

Root Number 18

pict

Meaning: to paint (from the Latin '*pictor*', '*pingere*')

'**Picture** yourself as a verbal genius, and you will increase the probability of becoming one!'

Example words

- **Pict**orial adjective. Relating to pictures.
  'She had a very pleasing and **pictorial** way of communicating ideas.'
- **Pict**ography noun. Picture writing.
  'Mind Maps may be considered a form of **pictography**.'
- **Pict**uresque adjective. Visually attractive in a charming manner –
  'just like a picture'.
  'It was one of the most beautiful and **picturesque** scenes on which
  they had ever set eyes.'

Root Number 19

put

Meaning: thinking, thought (from the Latin '*putare*', to think)

'With this handy little root you will be able to **compute** your grasp of
vocabulary progress, to win any **dispute** over its verification, and to
expand your growing **reputation** for Verbal Intelligence!'

Example words

- De**put**y noun. One appointed to think for another; a substitute.
  'Most good leaders choose a **deputy** to act in case of their
  absence.'
- Com**put**er noun. As you now know, this literally means 'with

word power I – roots: how to improve your
vocabulary, creativity, memory and IQ!

67

thinking', and describes a machine that thinks.

'The human bio-**computer** is significantly more intelligent than the silicone **computer**.'

- **Put**ative adjective. Generally considered, commonly thought, or reputed to be.

'Because it appeared that she was making a fortune, she was a **putative** millionaire.'

Root Number 20

soph

Meaning: wisdom (from the Greek 'sophia')

'This root will give you added **sophistication** in the use of language, and will help you in your pursuit of **philosophical** ideas.'

Example words

- **Soph**oclean adjective. Relating to the great Greek playwright and poet Sophocles, whose name means what he was called: 'The Wise One'.

'His writing was witty and weighty – almost Sophoclean in style.'
- **Soph**iology noun. The science of human ideas.

'Being interested in what the great minds of the past had thought about things, he decided to study **sophiology**.'
- **Soph**isticate noun. One who is discerning and aware of complex issues through education or experience.

'Her knowledge in many areas was superb; most people considered her a **sophisticate**.'

Root Number 21

tech

Meaning: skill or art (from the Greek '*technikos*')
    'This root will give you successful **techniques** for conversing with the **technocrats**!'

Example words

- Pyro**tech**nics noun. Literally, the fire skill or the fire art, especially fireworks.
  'New Year's Eve is a display-case for **pyrotechnics**.'
- **Tech**nocracy noun. Government by an élite of technical experts.
  '**Technocracy** is an oligarchy of those with specialized technical skills.'

Root Number 22

ultima

Meaning: last, final (from the Latin '*ultimas*')
    'You knew it! **Ultimately** we will have to come to the end of this particular, enjoyable venture. You are well on the way to **ultimate** success!'

---

word power I – roots: how to improve your vocabulary, creativity, memory and IQ!

69

Example words

- **Ultimo** adverb. Last month;the month preceding the present month.
  'This month I started my Verbal Intelligence development; **ultimo** I had not.'
- Pen**ultima**te adjective. Next to last.
  'Soon you will reach the **penultimate** root in this chapter!'
- **Ultima**te adjective. Last; final
  'Is man's **ultimate** destiny to populate the Universe?'

Root Number 23

ven   veni   vent

Meaning: come (from the Latin '*venere*')
  'This root will lead you to **eventful adventures**, helping to **intervene** between yourself and ignorance, and thus acting as **preventive** intellectual medicine! When you have mastered this and the other roots you will be able to say, as Julius Caesar did: "Veni. Vidi. Vice." "I came. I saw. I conquered."'

Example words

- **Vent**ure noun. A risky or daring journey, undertaking, or business enterprise.
  'They entered enthusiastically into their new **venture** together, convinced of their success.'

- **Vent**uresome adjective. Willing to take risks; bold; daring.
  'They were a **venturesome** bunch, and it was this very quality that drew people to them.'
- Ad**vent**itious adjective. Happening according to chance.
  'The sudden and unexpectedly large inheritance was an **adventitious** event that changed the family's fortunes.'

Root Number 24

ver   veri

Meaning: true; genuine (from the Latin '*verus*')

'When you have absorbed this root, you will be a voracious communicator, and will be very capable of **verifying** the truth in other people's statements.'

Example words

- **Ver**acity noun. Truth; honesty; accuracy.
  'He was an extremely ethical fellow, and spoke with complete sincerity and **veracity**.'
- **Veri**fy verb. To confirm; to prove to be true.
  'Before signing, I wish to **verify** that the contract is a true reflection of our spoken agreement.'
- **Veri**dical adjective. Truthful; veracious.
  'She had committed herself to tell the truth and did - hers was a completely **veridical** statement.'

---

word power I – roots: how to improve your vocabulary, creativity, memory and IQ!

71

Root Number 25

viv   vivi   vita

Meaning: alive; life (from the Latin '*vita*')

'This is a particularly important root that is **vital** to the development of your vocabulary, and will **vitalize** your spoken words as well as helping you to survive in any verbal situation!'

Example words

- **Vita**min noun. One of the constituents of food that are essential for life.
  'Many nutritionists recommend **vitamin** supplements to a regular diet in order to improve the quality of life.'
- **Viva**cious adjective. Full of energy, spirit and life.
  'Her sparkling, **vivacious** personality made her the belle of every ball.'
- **Vivi**parous adjective. Bearing live young (not eggs) that have been developed inside the body of the parent.
  'Human beings are **viviparous** creatures.'

Case Study – Notes for Words

Dr Agnes Chan, and her colleagues of the Chinese University of Hong Kong, have come up with an amazing finding: that children who take music lessons grow up to have a better memory for words. Chan's team found that women who had at least six years of music lessons before the age of 12, but who were not professional musicians, performed significantly better at standard word recall tests than women who had no musical training. Dr Chan believes that musical training could help everyone, including those with head injuries or learning difficulties, to improve their verbal intelligence.

These findings also confirm our growing knowledge of the fact that each one of our separate intelligences helps, supports and nurtures the others. In this instance Creative Intelligence (making music) is enhancing and improving Verbal Intelligence (word recall).

Case Study – How Do We Judge Intelligence in Strangers?

For many years, psychologists and others have been interested in the answer to this question. Some fascinating new light has been thrown onto the subject by Robert Gifford and D'Arcy Reynolds at the University of Victoria in British Columbia, Canada. Their research attempted to discover exactly which cues help us to judge IQ accurately, and which cues are not correlated with IQ.

Gifford and Reynolds videoed high-school students answering

word power I – roots: how to improve your vocabulary, creativity, memory and IQ!

73

thought-provoking questions such as: 'What do you see as the future of the world's environment?' Each of the students was also given standard IQ tests, and their IQs were logged.

The videos were then showed to a group of volunteers who became 'IQ judges'. These IQ judges were asked to watch the videos and then assess each student's body type and also to monitor a variety of behavioural cues, especially their verbal fluency; the number of different words they used; and how loudly they spoke. After they had completed this task, the judges were asked to rate the students' IQs.

The results?

Factors that had no relation to IQ included the following: halting speech; using slang; saying 'um'; being fat; talking loudly. It is interesting to note that this last one was often thought by the judges to be a sign of high intelligence!

The factors the judges rated as showing high intelligence, and which *were* directly correlated with the videoed students' IQs, were the following: *if a student was easy to understand; used a lot of words; or spoke quickly.*

The findings indicated that by training in these three areas, the standard IQ scores could rise.

verbal workout

Word Puzzle Number 5

1. zyglooo   __ X __ X __ __ X
2. chramon   __ __ __ X X __ X
3. phrag   __ __ __ X X
4. cectnon   __ X X __ __ __ X

Clue: Mind your body   __ __ __ __ __ __ __ __ __ __ __

Verbal Intelligence Tip

- When your eyes have 'absorbed' the letters of the puzzle, look away!

Why?

Because your brain has an 'inner screen' which it projects onto external reality, and onto this big blank screen your brain also projects the answer – much like your own virtual-reality blackboard, on which you can scribble notes that help you solve a problem.

This is why you often see young children, especially when they are asked to spell a word, look away. It is not because they are not paying attention; rather, they *are* paying attention – to that super-solution screen inside their heads.

Continuing to look at a puzzle, with your normal vision, keeps you 'small-screen' focused. Unless you have perceived the answer immediately, it is always best to bring the 'big screen' into play.

---

word power I – roots: how to improve your vocabulary, creativity, memory and IQ!

75

Word Puzzle Number 6

Ignorance is to not knowing as cognizant is to ...?

Surprise Yourself With Your Own Knowledge!

There is a wonderful confidence-building game you can play with your dictionary. Make sure you have a comprehensive dictionary such as the *Oxford English Dictionary* (OED), or perhaps the more American-slanted *Webster's Dictionary*.

Starting at the first word in the dictionary, go through, page by page, checking off the words you already know. Keep a little tally at the bottom of each page, as well as a running total indicating how many words you have identified so far that you know. This exercise can be done on a daily or weekly basis, or, if you feel like it, in large chunks (word bingeing!). You will find that you know many more words than you thought. In addition, you will discover many 'old friends' that for some reason have been put in the back of your mind. You can bring these to life once again, immediately adding to your total of current word-friends.

As you leaf through the pages, you will often spy tempting words that will beckon to you as you pass by. Be seduced! Go and visit them, and thus make even more friends.

Make Up New Words to Help You Remember

One new word can be the 'decoding device' that will enable your memory to recall, in perfect order, data that needs to be remembered in a given sequence. Perhaps one of the most common examples of this is the created name/character Roy Gbiv. He's a very colourful fellow: the letters of his name are the first letters for each of the colours of the rainbow, in order: Red, Orange, Yellow, Green, Blue, Indigo and Violet. If you have any that you have personally made up or use that you think would be helpful for future readers of *The Power of Verbal Intelligence*, please send them to me at the address on page 231.

Get a Thesaurus

As you may well know, it was one of the world's highest-ever Verbal Intelligences, Dr Samuel Johnson, who in the 18th century had the original idea of writing a book that listed all the main words in the known language, in conjunction with their meanings, parts of speech, most common usage and historical derivations. His brilliant first work, *The Dictionary of the English Language*, gave birth to all our modern dictionaries.

A few decades later, another man, Roget, had a similarly brilliant idea. He decided to write a book that also contained all of the words in the English language, but this time with a difference. Rather than giving the *meanings* of all the words, Roget's book would give all the words that had *similar* meanings to the given word.

Thus, for example, if you were writing a book, giving a speech or composing a poem, and wanted to have a variation on your theme, his book would give you every known 'companion word'. He called his book *Roget's Thesaurus*. Nearly every great writer and thinker has since used it, and it is a standard tool for all those who wish to improve their Verbal Intelligence, communication skills and ability.

---

word power I – roots: how to improve your vocabulary, creativity, memory and IQ!

77

Let's just look, for example, at just *some* of the entries in *Roget's Thesaurus* for the word 'intelligence':

Intelligence, wisdom: Mental Capacity. NOUNS

1. intelligence, understanding, Verstand [Ger.], comprehension, apprehension; savvy [slang, US]; sense, wit, mother wit, natural or native wit; intellect; **intellectuality**, intellectualism; **mentality**, rationality, intellectual power; capacity, caliber, reach or compass of mind; **I.Q.**, intelligence quotient, mental ratio, mental age; sanity; knowledge.

2. **smartness, braininess** [coll.], **brightness, brilliance, cleverness**, aptness, aptitude, native cleverness; sharpness, keenness, acuteness; quickness, nimbleness.

3. **sagacity**, sagaciousness, **astuteness, acumen**, gumption [coll. & dial.], flair; long head [coll.], longheadedness, hardheadedness

4. **wisdom**, wiseness, sageness, sapience, good or sound understanding; erudition

5. **sensibleness, reasonableness**, reason, rationality, sanity, saneness, soundness; sense, good ~ common or plain sense

6. **genius**, Geist [Ger.], spirit, soul; **inspiration**, afflatus, divine afflatus; fire of genius, lambent flame of intellect, coal from off the altar; talent; creative thought

Your Thesaurus, like your dictionary, will be your lifelong companion. Use them regularly to boost your Verbal Intelligence.

Use Your Favourite Words to Generate More Favourite Words

Make a list of your Top 10, or Top 100 favourite words. First use your dictionary to check their meanings (and especially derivations). Next go to your Thesaurus and check all those words that have similar meanings to your favourite words. As you explore you will find many new friends, who will become both new favourites and will enhance your growing vocabulary.

Learn Five New Word Roots Each Year

Give yourself the simple task of learning five new word roots each year. You can do this in concentrated chunks, or spread them out over the seasons. It may not sound like much, but after 10 years you will have acquired *150 new roots, which, themselves, will help you generate thousands of new words.*

Look For Onomatopoeic Words and Phrases

Onomatopoeia, as you know, is a word or phrase that sounds like the thing it describes. Two well-known examples are 'the murmuring of innumerable bees', and 'the tintinnabulation of tiny bells'. Onomatopoeic words add power, rhythm and beauty to your growing vocabulary and communication skills.

Word Power Booster Number 3

This Word Power Booster is devoted to words that themselves suggest power and strength. When you use them it will similarly add power and strength to your vocabulary and power and strength to your Verbal

word power I – roots: how to improve your
vocabulary, creativity, memory and IQ!

79

Intelligence. Chose the definition you think is closest to the actual meaning of each word. The answers are on page 217 – 18.

1 INTREPID (in-*tré*-pid)
    (a) Terrified
    (b) In-between
    (c) Strong
    (d) Fearless

2 IMPREGNABLE (im-*prég*-nabul)
    (a) Not pregnant
    (b) Cannot be taken
    (c) Infertile
    (d) Of great magnitude

3 UNALTERABLE (un-*órter*-abul)
    (a) An argument
    (b) Incapable of religious conversion
    (c) Unable to be changed
    (d) Changeable

4 PARAMOUNT (*pá*-rra-mount)
    (a) A film
    (b) To ascend a peak
    (c) A small mountain
    (d) Of chief importance

the power of verbal intelligence

5 RIGOROUS (*ríg*-or-rus)

   (a) Flexible
   (b) Exacting
   (c) Sickly
   (d) Like rope

6 UNMITIGATED (un-*mít*-igay-ted)

   (a) Unqualified
   (b) Unexamined
   (c) Unfenced; free
   (d) Not met

7 CLIMACTIC (cly-*mák*-tic)

   (a) Meteorological
   (b) To ascend
   (c) Reaching the highest point
   (d) Equatorial

8 SACROSANCT (*sákro*-sankt)

   (a) Most sacred; inviolable
   (b) Sugar-like
   (c) A mortuary
   (d) Impossible

9 UNIMPEACHABLE (un-im-*péech*-abul)

   (a) Not allowed to sell fruit

word power I – roots: how to improve your
vocabulary, creativity, memory and IQ!

81

(b) Not pleasant

(c) Unable to be called into question; irreproachable

(d) Extremely pleasant

10 CLARION (*klár*-ion)

(a) A small clarinet

(b) Loud and clear

(c) A household cleaner

(d) A gong

chapter four

'So long as the language lives then the nation lives too.'

Czech proverb

Words are power. Words are wealth. Words are your Intellectual Capital, the currency with which you communicate, relate to those around you, do business, express your full range of feelings from anger to love, create your personal literature, persuade, influence, guide others, and direct your own life.

Case Study – Verbal Intelligence and Academic Success

Dr Wilfred Funk reports on an experiment on vocabulary improvement and academic success, which was carried out in two American school classes. The ages and background of the two groups of students were similar and each contained a similar cross-section of the local community.

One class carried on with its normal studies. The second group of students, the 'experimental group', were given extra classes, in which they had special and rigorous training to develop their vocabulary and Verbal Intelligence.

As you might expect, at the end of the study the students who had had Verbal Intelligence training scored higher marks in English tests than did the 'control group'.

However, far more significant than this was the fact that they scored higher marks in *every other subject*, including all the sciences and mathematics!

Improving Verbal Intelligence has a dramatic and positive effect on all aspects of academic success.

Case Study – Word Power, Hats and Stockings!

Dr Funk reports two other experiments that demonstrate the power of the word, both involving word power and fashion.

The first experiment involved men and a store's hat department. Two counters in the department were covered with identical numbers of identical hats, each hat being of the same make, and the styles and colours on each counter being exactly the same.

The only difference between the two counters was that on one there was printed the large word 'Tyrolean'. The other counter had no sign.

Do you think this single word had any effect on sales and, if so, how much?

The amazing result was that *three times* as many of the 'worded' hats were sold!

The second experiment involved women, fashion and a similar experimental design.

This time, two counters were stocked with identical brands and styles of plain beige stockings.

As with the hat experiment, the two counters were identical, except that on one the stockings were labelled 'Gala', and the other had no sign at all. *Ten times* as many pairs of the Gala stockings were sold!

Store up these experiments in your Verbal Intelligence databanks. Realize how much power your words have to influence others. Realize also how much power words have to influence you!

'Words are the pegs on which to hang ideas.'

(Henry Ward Beecher)

A single word or phrase can multiply sales, mend a fractured relationship, inspire a nation, immortalize a name and change history.

The otherwise relatively unknown English poet Stevie Smith is known to increasing millions for the brilliant and moving end to one of her poems:

'I was much too far out all my life
And not waving but drowning.'

John F. Kennedy changed the focus of the American nation, and the perception and direction of the human race, with his immortal statement in 1961 to put an American on the moon within 10 years:

'I believe that the nation should commit itself to achieving the goal, before this decade is out, of landing a man on the moon and returning him safely to the earth.'

Similarly, the careless use of a phrase can dog an individual for the rest of his life. Many of you reading this book will know who said the phrase: 'I didn't inhale.' This unfortunate choice of words will haunt Bill Clinton for decades.

word beginnings and word endings

You are now about to embark on another adventure similar to that on which you embarked with Roots. This time you will explore the universe of Prefixes (word beginnings) and Suffixes (word endings) – 12 in all. These are like Roots that exist at the beginning and ends of words. Once again, you will be entertained by the Ancient Romans and Greeks. They will help you on your way to developing a rich and robust vocabulary.

Enjoy the journey!

Case Study – Vocabulary and Standard IQ

The great IQ guru, Professor Lewis M. Turman of Stanford University, posed an interesting question. He wanted to know if vocabulary tests alone would be as accurate an indicator of intelligence as full-blown IQ tests, which would include, in addition, logical and mathematical questions, etc. He found that they did! Turman had discovered that vocabulary alone was an extremely successful indicator of academic and professional success and overall standard intelligence.

Prefix Number 1

con-   co-

Meaning: with; together (from the Latin)

'This prefix will allow you to make good **connections** when other people who love language **congregate**.'

Example words

- **Con**gress noun. The act of coming together; a meeting.
  'A number of nations call the place where their top politicians come together **Congress**.'
- **Co-**operation noun. To operate together; a joint effort or labour.
  '**Co-operation** with nature has been found to be the best means of survival.'
- **Con**sanguineous adjective. Denotes people who are 'together' in that they are of the same blood/family.

'The two strangers discovered to their amazement that they were **consanguineous**.'

Prefix Number 2

dyn-

Meaning: power (from the Greek '*dunamis*')
    'This prefix will help you become even more **dynamic** in your use of words, and people will probably start referring to you as "a real **dynamo**"!'

Example words

- **Dyn**asty noun. An especially powerful line of kings or rulers.
  'The Kennedy clan in America is an example of a modern political **dynasty**.'
- **Dyn**amism noun. The quality of power, energy and forcefulness.
  'His deep knowledge and passionate love of the subject enabled him to speak with exceptional **dynamism**.'
- **Dyn**amo noun. A device that produces electrical energy.
  'He was so full of energy – a real **dynamo**.'

Prefix Number 3

eu-

Meaning: pleasant; well; good (from the Greek '*eus*')

'This prefix will hopefully have you in a state of euphoria, exclaiming, as you discover more and more, "**Eureka**"!'

Example words

- **Eu**phemism noun. The use of a mild or more pleasant word in place of one that is more blunt and harsh.
  'Because she didn't want to insult him, she used "ample" as a **euphemism** to describe his obese body!'
- **Eu**pepsia noun. Good digestion.
  'A healthy diet, good exercise and a happy state of mind should promote **eupepsia**.'
- **Eu**phonious adjective. Full of pleasant and pleasing sound; harmonious.
  'Lying in a meadow on a spring day, the lovers listened to the **euphonious** music of Nature.'

Prefix Number 4

phil-

Meaning: love (from the Greek '*philos*', loving)

'By the time you have finished reading *The Power of Verbal Intelligence*, you will be a **philologist**, for you will have become a student, scholar and lover of language.'

Example words

- **Phil**osophy noun. The love of wisdom and the study of the fundamental nature of knowledge, existence and reality.
  'Everyone has been a student of **philosophy**, for at some times in our lives we all ask "what's the point of it all?"!'
- **Phil**anthropist noun. A lover of humankind; a generous giver to good causes.
  'One of the greatest **philanthropists** in history was Andrew Carnegie, who amassed a fortune when young, and spent the rest of his life giving it away to charitable causes.'
- **Phil**omath noun. A lover of learning.
  'The **philomath** adored finding out new and unusual things.'

Prefix Number 5

prim-   prime-

Meaning: first (from the Latin '*primus*')
  '*The Power of Verbal Intelligence* is a **primer** designed **primarily** to introduce you to the wonderful world of words!'

Example words

- **Prime**val adjective. Belonging to the first ages of the earth.
  'The **primeval** forests still exist today, in the form of either

archaeological imprints or coal and oil.'

- **Prim**ates noun. The first, 'highest' order of mammals, consisting of man and the apes.
  'Studies of the other **primates** show that they are far more intelligent than previously thought.'
- **Prim**acy noun. State of being first.
  'The **primacy** effect states that human beings tend to remember the first things they come across.'

Prefix Number 6

tra- trans-

Meaning: across, through or over (from the Latin)
  'This prefix crops up a lot in the world of **travel**. Think of some examples, and keep your eye out for more the next time you are in **transit**!'

Example words

- **Trans**cend verb. To cross to a higher level.
  'The music **transcended** anything she had heard before.'
- **Tra**verse verb. Lying across.
  'The new bridge will **traverse** the river.'
- **Trans**action noun. Putting through a business deal; passing goods 'across' from one person to another.
  'After much negotiation, they completed a successful transaction.'

Suffix Number 1

-able   -ible

Meaning: able; can do (from the Latin suffix '*-aiblis*', '*-ibilis*', meaning suitable for the purpose indicated)

'With this **incredible** suffix you will be **capable** of expanding your vocabulary to the extent that you will be considered most **able** by everyone who comes in contact with you.'

Example words

- Soci**able** adjective. Possessing Social Intelligence; able to get along with people.
  'He was a **sociable** person, which made him very popular.'
- Ed**ible** adjective. Can be eaten.
  'Apples, pears and bananas are all **edible** fruits.'
- Enjoy**able** adjective. Able to be relished or enjoyed.
  'Things which appeal to our senses tend to be **enjoyable**.'
- Ten**able** adjective. That which can be defended or maintained, especially an argument (from the French '*tenir*', to build).
  'Because his arguments were so **tenable**, the scholarship committee made his appointment **tenable** for seven years.'

Suffix Number 2

-ic

Meaning: like; nature of (from the Greek '*ikos*')

'This suffix often has -ally added to it; a fact which I wish to state **emphat-ically**!'

Example words

- Hero**ic** adjective. Like a hero.
  'It was a feat of **heroic** proportions.'
- Majest**ic** adjective. Like royalty.
  'He strode **majestically** into the room.'
- Endem**ic** adjective. Native to a particular people or area.
  'The panda is **endemic** to China.'

Suffix Number 3

-ity

Meaning: a state of or quality (from the Latin '*-itas*')

'The more you develop your verbal **ability**, the more you will be able to speak with **clarity**, **dignity** and **authority**. No one will ever accuse you of unnecessary **ambiguity** or verbal **absurdity**!'

---

word power II – prefixes and suffixes

Example words

- Luminos**ity** noun. Brilliance; the state of having a great deal of radiance or light.
  'The spacecraft shone with an eerie **luminosity**.'
- Etern**ity** noun. State of timelessness; time never ending.
  'Infinity is to distance as **eternity** is to time.'
- Celer**ity** noun. The quality of quickness; speed.
  'She spoke with incredible **celerity**, yet with equal clarity.'

Suffix Number 4

–ize   -ise

Meaning: to make or become (from the Latin suffix '-*izare*')
'This suffix will **familiarize** you with and **acclimatize** you to a whole range of words that will help you to **emphasize** your point!'

Example words

- Memor**ize** verb. To establish strongly and to make firm in the mind.
  'The Mind Map is a thinking tool that will help you to **memorize** whatever you wish to learn.'
- Mesmer**ize** verb. To make someone hypnotized or spell-bound. (After Anton Mesmer, who was the first to publicize hypnosis.)
  'My gripping tales will **mesmerize** you!'
- Scrutin**ize** verb. To make a close examination.

'Before signing anything significant, it is always best to **scrutinize** the small print.'

Suffix Number 5

-ology

Meaning: the subject of study; a science (from the Latin '*logia*')

'With this new suffix and with your growing knowledge of other suffixes, you are already well on your way to being a **philologist**!'

Example words

- Ethn**ology** noun. The study of the races of humankind.
  'In recent years **ethnology** has become a newly popular science, as humankind search for their geographic and racial origins.'
- Eth**ology** noun. The study of the behaviour of animals.
  'In the middle of the 20th century researchers began to realize all animals were far more intelligent and individually unique than had been previously thought. They thus started to investigate, and founded the science of **ethology**.'
- Phil**ology** noun. The study of words and languages.
  'As you have been reading *The Power of Verbal Intelligence*, you have been studying **philology**!'

Suffix Number 6

-ous

Meaning: full of or having (from the Latin '-osus')

'With your increased Verbal Intelligence it is **obvious** that your appetite for learning will be **voracious** and that others will consider your verbal skills **wondrous**!'

Example words

- Lusci**ous** adjective. Having a taste and/or smell that is rich, full and delicious.
  'The exquisitely prepared meal was one of the most **luscious** they had ever experienced.'
- Mysteri**ous** adjective. Full of obscurity; mystery.
  'Scientists who study the Universe proclaim that, despite our growing knowledge, it still remains **mysterious**.'
- Noxi**ous** adjective. Unpleasant; harmful; poisonous
  'The children mixed up a **noxious**-smelling brew in their chemistry lesson.'

verbal workout

Word Puzzle Number 7

1. pudety   __ X X __ __ __
2. vitacree   __ __ X X __ __ __ X
3. naribs   __ X X __ __ X
4. hekish   X X __ __ X __

Clue: Ultimate wordsmith   _ _ _ _ _ _ _ _ _ _

Verbal Intelligence Tip

■ Close your eyes while contemplating the word puzzle.
Why?

Once again the answer lies in your brain's remarkable ability to create a
virtual screen, this time inside your head. When your eyes are closed,
your brain no longer has to deal with the visual data that pours in
when your eyes are open. It can therefore concentrate even more fully
on the problem at hand, and will project a correct answer more rapidly
onto its internal screen. The sudden rest that your eyes get often acts
like a sudden release of energy (which it is), which is immediately
poured into finding the answer you are seeking.

Word Puzzle Number 8

Hating mankind is to misanthropy as loving mankind is to ...?

---

word power II – prefixes and suffixes

Word Power Booster Number 4

In this Word Power Booster you will be thinking about thinking! All the words are concerned with the theories about who, what and why we are. Choose the definition that you think is closest to the correct meaning from the four options given.

1 ATHEIST (*áy*-thee-ist)
   (a) Belief that God is non-existent
   (b) Uncertainty about God
   (c) Believer in God
   (d) One who does not care about God

2 AGNOSTIC (ag-*nóss*-tic)
   (a) Belief that God is non-existent
   (b) Uncertainty about God
   (c) Believer in God
   (d) One who does not care about God

3 ALTRUISM (*ál*-tru-ism)
   (a) Belief in a higher power
   (b) Mountaineering
   (c) Generous and unselfish
   (d) Believing in honesty

4 EGOIST (*ée*-go-ist)

    (a) Belief in a single God

    (b) Traveller

    (c) Fighter

    (d) One interested in selfish advantage

5 EPICURE (*épi*-kure)

    (a) Treatment for the hands

    (b) One who loves good food; a gourmet

    (c) Cure for disease

    (d) Centre of activity

6 FATALIST (*fáte*-a-list)

    (a) One who always wins

    (b) One who always loses

    (c) One who always gives up

    (d) One who believes that events are determined by fate

7 LIBERAL (*líb*-er-al)

    (a) A believer in progress

    (b) Poor

    (c) Liking books

    (d) Military officer

8 CONSERVATIVE (con-*súrv*-a-tif)

    (a) Similar to Liberal

    (b) Environmentalist

    (c) A believer in familiar traditions

    (d) Agriculturalist

9 STOIC (*stów*-ik)

    (a) Alien

    (b) Able to endure pain and hardship without complaining

    (c) One who hoards

    (d) Similar to Epicure

10 CHAUVINISM (*shów*-vin-ism)

    (a) Lover of French

    (b) Lover of horses

    (c) Extreme lover of one's country

    (d) Singer of French songs

brain word –

using your brain power to develop your word power

chapter five

'Your boss has a bigger vocabulary than you have. That's one good reason why he's your boss.'

Dr Wilfred Funk and Dr Norman Lewis

In this chapter I will introduce you to the amazing nature of words and their incredible ability to multiply themselves, your Creativity and your Verbal Intelligence.

Your memory is vitally important in the development of your vocabulary. I will show you how to master your memory functions to help accelerate the growth of your Verbal Intelligence.

Then I will show you how to combine the powers of your left and right brains to increase the power of your vocabulary, and how to combine everything you have learned in *The Power of Verbal Intelligence* so far to create those thinking tools – Mind Maps.

the multi-ordinate nature of words

I hope by now you have raced to your dictionary in order to check out the meaning and derivation of the word 'multi-ordinate'! The derivation of the two-part word is as follows: the prefix 'multi' comes from the Latin *'multus'*, meaning 'much' or 'many'. The word 'ordinate' comes from the Latin *'ordo'*, meaning 'order'.

So, the multi-ordinate nature of words refers to the fact that they do not have only one meaning in your brain – they radiate out from their centre with many orders of meaning.

Can we demonstrate this?

Yes!

On page 106 you will find the word 'Power' in the centre of a page, with 10 branches radiating from it. As fast as you can, print, clearly, on the lines, the first 10 words that come into your mind when you think of the word 'Power'. If you have friends or family with you, get them to do the same exercise, but separately from you. You do not want anybody to see what the others have done until everyone has completed the exercise. Do this now, and then read on.

On page 109 I have completed the same exercise. Check your own words against mine, seeing how many are identical (i.e., the same meaning, and exactly the same spelling).

If you are doing this exercise with friends, take it in turn to read your words out to the others. As each person reads, the others note down all the words, each person therefore ending up with the entire collection. See how many words are common to all of you, or to any sub-group of you.

In 999 cases out of 1,000, there are *very* few words in common.

What does this mean? It means that your vocabulary is much more expansive than you previously thought, that your ability to make associations is potentially infinite (you could have added 10 additional associations to every one of your 10 prime ordinals, couldn't you? And so on!)

It further means that your own associations are unique, and that *your ability to grow your vocabulary and enhance your Verbal Intelligence is infinite.*

Case Study – Translate and Beware!

The multi-faceted wonder of words can often lead to hilarious mistranslations or misunderstandings. A recent issue of *New Scientist* magazine reported some wonderful bloopers:

One reader reported that the radio station The Voice of America, used to transmit western news and propaganda to the Soviet Bloc. They would then listen to the various countries' re-translations of their transmissions. One news item reported the death of a former tennis champion, who died at her home in Tooting, London. Bulgarian radio broadcast the fact that she had: 'Died at her home in London, playing her trumpet!'

Another reader reported the story of a computer-translated Russian technical article, converted into English. The confused engineers reading it could not make sense of the frequently recurring references to 'water goats'. After a lot of thinking, the solution dawned: 'water goats' were 'hydraulic rams'!

This last story is reminiscent of one of the oldest translation/re-translation stories, also from Russian to English. 'Out of sight, out of mind' was reborn as 'invisible idiot'!

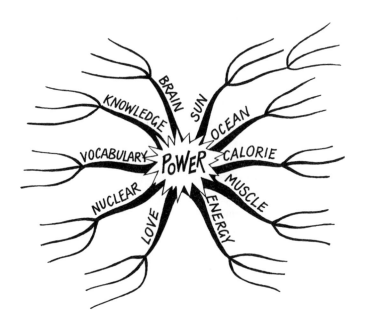

memory and verbal intelligence –
recall during learning

Research from the time of Hermann Ebbinghaus and William James at the end of the 19th century, to the current work of Professor Guttmann of Vienna University and myself, has confirmed that the patterns of memory are stable, predictable and, most importantly, *manageable*.

Research has confirmed that while you are learning, you will remember more the following things:

- The beginning of the learning period (the Primacy Effect)
- The end of the learning period (the Recency Effect)
- Anything that stands out in your *imagination*
- Anything that you *associate* with something else

memory – recall after learning

Again, research has consistently confirmed the same findings about what happens to your recall after you have finished learning something (some people call this 'forgetting'!).

There is a simple formula to keep your memory sharp rather than letting it drop off calamitously. The first part of the formula is *Repetition*. You must repeat something at least five times for it to sink into your long-term memory. The second part is the timing or spacing of those five repetitions.

Your repetitions, or reviews, should be spaced out roughly according to the following formula:

- First repetition – after one hour
- Second repetition – after one day
- Third repetition – after one week
- Fourth repetition – after one month
- Fifth repetition – after six months

Following this formula for your Verbal Intelligence studies will make the difference between complete success and absolute failure.

your left and right brain

Less than 20 years ago, most people had never heard of the left/right brain research. Now, fortunately, it has become part of global knowledge.

To summarize briefly: the left side of your brain deals predominantly with words, logic, numbers, sequence, linearity, analysis and lists. The right side of your brain deals predominantly with rhythm, spatial awareness, dimension, imagination, daydreaming, colour and holistic awareness.

You will see that words are designated to belong on the left side of the brain. This, however, is not the final picture. For people with high Verbal Intelligences, brainwave measurements show that when they are presented with words the whole cortex lights up. In other words, words are everywhere! This is especially true of poets, writers and Grandmasters of Memory.

The reason their entire brains light up is because they realize that words are not simply words. Words are the word itself *plus the imaginative, colourful, rhythmical and spatial associations that are part of the full meaning of that word!*

mind maps

Mind Maps are perfect examples of the above principle.

They are an explosion of the multi-ordinate nature of words exercise

---

you did with 'Power'. Their key is that any word or image can be placed in the centre of the page, and can radiate out infinitely.

Mind Maps® are also an exact reflection of the Recall During Learning principles of Association and Imagination. Indeed you could describe a Mind Map as an *associative* network of images (*imagination*) and words.

Further, Mind Maps® incorporate all the elements of your left and right brain, giving you the added power of the synergy between the two sides (the 1 + 1 = more than 2 principle).

By using Mind Maps® you vastly enhance your Verbal Intelligence. There are colourful examples of Mind Maps® in the plate section.

verbal workout

Word Puzzle Number 9

1. hacyt	__ X __ __ __
2. volen	X X __ __ __
3. ryemom	__ __ __ X X __
4. ziliode	__ X __ X __ __ X

Clue: Brain of the millennium. __ __ __ __ __ __ __ __

- Look at the jumbled letters in 'soft focus'.

Why?

Because soft focus once again allows your para-conscious brain to work on the problem.

Soft focus is when you 'let your eyes go', much as if you are too tired to focus, or as if you are 'looking beyond' the letters in front of you. When you do this the letters become a little bit fuzzy (you are literally using 'fuzzy logic' here!) and tend to shift or wobble about in your visual field. This gets them out of the rigid order that they are in on the page, and allows your brain to play around with them much more freely. Because this is happening, you are much more likely to have the answer 'pop up'. This is also because your brain, scanning the way in which the fuzzy images are appearing, can more easily see appropriate patterns of letters as they shift around in front of your eyes.

It is a paradoxical situation, worth giving some thought to, that in this instance clarity keeps you farther away from the correct answer, while fuzziness gives you clarity!

Word Puzzle Number 10

Which is the odd one out?

- GORENNIT
- MILEHU
- GRETI
- NEXGYO

Understanding Understanding and Misunderstanding!

Next time you have a disagreement with a friend or colleague, just remember the 'multi-ordinate' nature of words. Rather than misunderstanding the disagreement from your set of verbal associations, and therefore getting yourself stressed out, calm yourself down, and set about exploring the universe of *their* associations.

In more than 90 per cent of the time you will find that not only were the misunderstandings understandable; you both end up agreeing that each of you had a good perspective on the situation at the time. This is much more productive, leads to much greater Creativity, and causes far less pain than sticking to the one-sided (and verbally unintelligent) assumption that you are absolutely right!

One of the best ways to explore your differences is to brainstorm with Mind Maps®. First do a Mind Map® of one side of the 'argument', then a Mind Map® of the other. These two Mind Maps® allow you to explore your differences objectively and effectively, and to create a third Mind Map®, which records your conclusions and your joint excellence!

Such an approach reduces stress levels and keeps you far more cheerful and healthy!

Use the 'Recall During Learning' Principles

Apply the 'Recall During Learning' Principles to help you continue to improve your Verbal Intelligence:

- Study in 20–40-minute time periods to help you maximize your recall, and to give you more Primacy and Recency Effects

- Actively look for new associations between words, using Mind Map® techniques and brainstorming
- Make the new words you learn 'outstanding' in your brain, by speaking them loudly, writing them large and highlighting them in any way you can.

Use the 'Recall After Learning' Principles

Apply the 'Recall After Learning' Principles to help you improve and maintain your Word Power.

Enter into your diary the dates when you will be working specifically on your Verbal Intelligence, as well as those dates when you plan to have special review sessions either with by yourself or with friends. Make sure your study and review dates fit in perfectly with the Recall After Learning Principles explained on page 110. If you do this you will get double the benefit from the same amount of time spent improving your Verbal Intelligence.

Highlight Key Words

Whenever you are studying *anything*, highlight the important key words as you read. By highlighting words like this, ideally with a highlighter-pen or a computer-screen enhancing device, you will be using the von Restorff Effect to your great benefit, and will be improving both your memory and your ability to 'swing into action' with your new words.

The principle of the von Restorff Effect is that anything that is unusual, colourful or humorous is far more easily remembered and

---

recalled by the brain than things which are plain and boring. This is just how Mind Maps® work!

Use Your Imagination and Daydream!

Apply the right-brain skills of 'Imagination' and 'Daydreaming' to the enhancement of your Verbal Intelligence. Occasionally daydream about yourself in situations where your verbal skills are giving full range to your full verbal potential. Imagine yourself writing superb letters, poems, reports and novels; imagine yourself making speeches that are mesmerizing in their power and verbal excellence; imagine yourself on TV, wowing the millions with your wit and eloquence.

When you daydream with intention, you increase the probability that what you daydream will come true. It is also fun!

You can also use your imagination to enhance your understanding and memory of new words. Let's imagine that you never fully understood the word 'sumptuous'.

To remember this word, rather than simply committing to memory the dictionary definition, it would be far better to *imagine* all kinds of glorious situations in which the word 'sumptuous' would apply – the richest, most lavish environments you can imagine, like those in the *Arabian Nights*, or feasts in the castles and palaces of world leaders. And don't simply daydream – really put yourself in them! Again, much more effective and much more fun!

Constantly bear in mind that words are a combination of the derivation, spelling and dictionary definition of the word, *plus* the vast storehouse of your imaginative, colourful, rhythmical and other multiple associations.

When you do this, your vocabulary will grow in size, richness and wealth.

Use Colour and Rhythm

Use the right-brain skills of 'colour' and 'rhythm' to develop your Verbal Intelligence. Imagine colours associated with the meanings of words; imagine words as colour; underline notes in different colours for different purposes (for example: red for action; blue for further thought, etc.), and highlight them in the same manner. These are all right-brain techniques you can use to increase your Word Power.

Similarly, applying rhythm and rhyme to the acquisition and use of words will also help. The reason why young children love nursery rhymes so much is that nursery rhymes give them a double dose of rhythm and rhyme, making the 'game of learning' much more easy and fun.

In the same way, great poets add considerable power to the messages they are trying to convey, by using appropriate rhythm and brain-jolting rhyme. A good example of this is from Lord Byron's *Childe Harold's Pilgrimage*, in which he is trying to convey the tremendous power of the ocean in comparison to the boasted but relatively minor power of mankind's navies:

Roll on, thou deep and dark blue Ocean – roll!
Ten thousand fleets sweep over thee in vain.

Mind Map Your Progress

Taking one or two main themes from each of the first four chapters, create a Mind Map® that summarizes what you have learned so far, and what general and specific progress you have made developing your Verbal Intelligence. You will be impressed with yourself! Your Verbal IQ is on the rise!

Word Power Booster Number 5

We are going to breathe spirit into your vocabulary as well enlarging it. I am going to introduce you to words based on the Latin root *'anima'*, meaning mind, breath, soul or spirit, and the Latin *'magnus'*, which as you know, means large. Once again, choose the definition that you think is closest to the correct meaning from the four options given (answers on page 220 – 221).

1 ANIMATE (*án*-ee-mayte)
   (a)   Like an animal
   (b)   Frantic
   (c)   Dumb
   (d)   To invest with life

2 UNANIMOUS (yu-*nán*-ee-mus)
   (a)   One animal
   (b)   Generally agreed
   (c)   Agreed by all
   (d)   Not agreed

3 MAGNANIMOUS (mag-*nán*-ee-mus)
   (a) Generous and forgiving
   (b) Big and powerful
   (c) Magnetic animal
   (d) Extinct animal

4 EQUANIMITY (ek-wa-*ním*-i-tee)
   (a) Relating to the Equator
   (b) Similar breed of animal
   (c) Water animal
   (d) Calmness; composure

5 ANIMADVERT (a-*ním*-ad-vert)
   (a) Inadvertent
   (b) Animal poster
   (c) Turn one's mind to; consider critically
   (d) Invest with spirit

6 MAGNATE (*mág*-nayte)
   (a) Metal that attracts metal
   (b) Important person in industry
   (c) Fat person
   (d) Big building

7 MAGNILOQUENT (mag-*ní-lok*went)

  (a) Using flowery language
  (b) Possessing a big mouth
  (c) A magnetic liquid
  (d) Speaking badly about others

8 MAGNIFICENCE (mag-*niff*-isense)

  (a) Putting boundaries on magnets
  (b) Greatness; grandeur
  (c) Aristocratic
  (d) Gross

9 MAGNUM OPUS (*mág*-num o-pus)

  (a) Large bottle of Champagne
  (b) Big business man
  (c) Gigantic building
  (d) Great literary or artistic work

10 MAGNUM (*mág*-num)

  (a) A boss
  (b) A large building
  (c) A wine bottle twice the standard size
  (d) A king

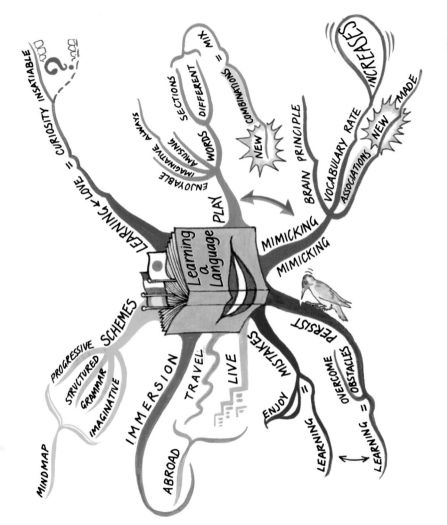

MINDMAP

SCHEMES
PROGRESSIVE
STRUCTURED
GRAMMAR
IMAGINATIVE

IMMERSION

ABROAD

TRAVEL

LIVE

MISTAKES

ENJOY

LEARNING =

LEARNING

OVERCOME OBSTACLES

PERSIST

MIMICKING

MIMICKING

LEARNING = LOVE → CURIOSITY INSATIABLE

PLAY

ENJOYABLE
AMUSING
IMAGINATIVE
ALWAYS
WORDS
SECTIONS
DIFFERENT

= MIX

NEW COMBINATIONS

BRAIN PRINCIPLE

VOCABULARY RATE

ASSOCIATIONS

NEW MADE

INCREASES

Learning a Language

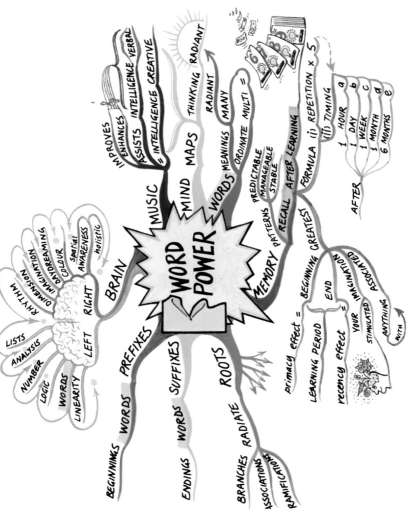

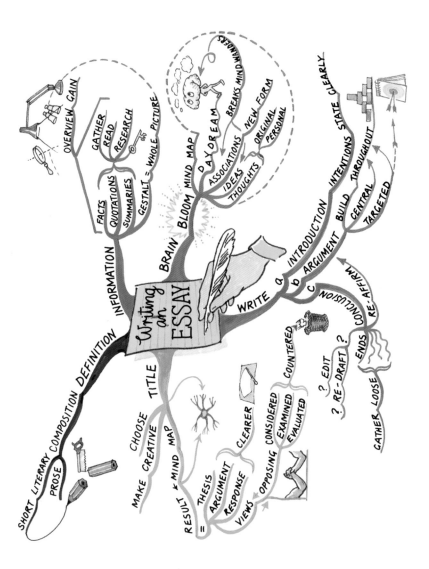

Summary Mind-Map® of Chapter 5

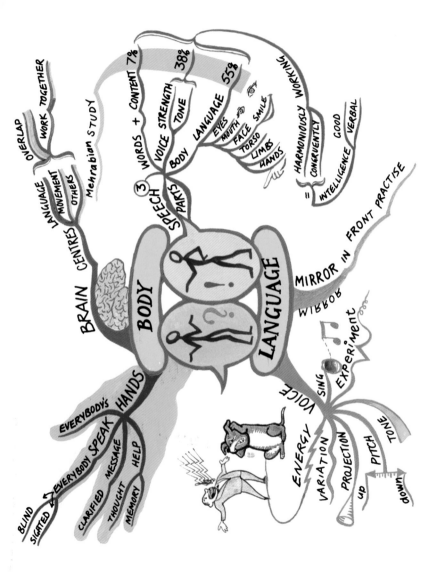

PREPARING FOR A JOB INTERVIEW

WHY ? THIS JOB

AFTER LETTER
THANKS
CONFIRMED
INTEREST FURTHER
INFORMATION

COMPANY RESEARCH
WHAT ATTRACTS
EXPECTED
UNDERSTAND
PAST
FUTURE

YOU
QUALIFICATIONS
TRAINING
EXPERIENCE

RELEVANT
USEFUL

PERSONALITY DISPLAY
POSITIVE ONLY
EMPLOYERS OTHER

LOUDLY
CONFIDENTLY
RESERVEDLY
EXPERIENCES
AMBITIONS
ACHIEVEMENTS
SPEAK

SHOW
ENTHUSIASM
VIVIDLY
VARIED TONE

AIMS: BE ENTERTAINING
UNDERSTOOD
QUOTABLE
REMEMBERED:
FIRST IMPRESSION
LAST
STRONGEST

HOBBIES
PROFESSIONAL
LEISURE
ARTISTIC
SPORTING
CULTURAL

INTERESTS

PREPARE
QUESTIONS
ANSWERS

JOB
SCHOOL SUBJECTS
BEST
JOBS LAST : LEFT WHY?
FIRED EVER? WHY?
AMBITIONS GOALS

DAY
DRESS APPROPRIATE GROOM
? FORMAL
? INFORMAL

REMEMBER
WHAT SAID
JOB
APPLICATION

BE INTERVIEW
PUNCTUAL!
DELAY
PREPARED
BOOK TAKE
RELAX

SMILE GREET
ATTENTIVE POSTURE
RELAXED
ALERT

Summary Mind-Map® of Chapter 8

Summary MindMap® of Chapter 10

chapter six

'Let your own discretion be your tutor: suit the action to the word, the word to the action.'

William Shakespeare, *Hamlet*

'He who knows that power is unborn ... and so perceiving, throws himself unhesitatingly on his thought, instantly rights himself, stands in the erect position, commands his limbs, works miracles.'

Ralph Waldo Emerson

Your body is a major part of your Verbal Intelligence!

This statement might have seemed ridiculous even a few years ago. Now, however, with our knowledge of our multiple intelligences and how they each integrate with each other, we have come to realize that we have disconnected our Verbal Intelligence from our bodies, to our own great disadvantage.

We will now reconnect them!

The major part of your Verbal Intelligence, the part that is spoken, has your body as its main constituent.

When you express your Verbal Intelligence with spoken words, there is not one, but three parts to the expression of this intelligence:

1. Your words and their content
2. Your voice and its strength and tone
3. Your body and its language

The perfect expression of Verbal Intelligence takes place when all three of these elements are working in perfect harmony, and are completely congruent.

When they are not congruent, Verbal Intelligence is literally dis-integrated and weak.

the sound of silence

Albert Mehrabian, in his work *Silent Messages*, revealed a fascinating study on the relationship between the three elements of spoken Verbal Intelligence.

Mehrabian discovered that, *especially when there was incongruity in the message*, those receiving it gave the following emphasis to each element in terms of their judgement whether the message was true or not:

Words and content	7%
Voice tone and energy	38%
Body and its language	55%

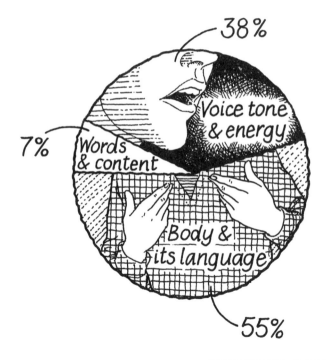

the power of verbal intelligence

Why was it that Mehrabian achieved this incredible result?

Because people receiving your Verbal Intelligence know that your body will show what your imagination is picturing, and what your true feelings are. In the same way, your tone of voice will also reveal what you are really imagining and feeling.

It is quite possible for you to recite words without meaning them. It is much more difficult to falsify the language with your body and the tone and energy of your voice.

True Verbal Intelligence, in its spoken manifestation, is where the imagination fires the body and voice so that these two magnificent instruments add meaning, weight and body to the skeleton of the isolated words.

In this situation it is impossible to divide them into percentages, for they become One whole.

Case Study – I've Got to Hand It to You!

Why is it that no matter where you go in the world, and no matter what the nationality, language, sex or age of the speaker, all humans speak with their hands? Jana Iverson, of Indiana University in Bloomington, and Susan Goldin-Meadow at the University of Chicago, decided to find out why it is that we wave our hands about so much when we talk to each other.

One possible explanation is that all our gestures come from mimicking our parents and people around us as we grow up. Iverson and Goldin-Meadow put this to the test with an ingenious experiment. They took 12 young people aged between 8 and 18, half of whom were blind from birth. They were all asked to perform a simple task: to pour water from a tall, slim glass into a short, flat dish. When they had completed the task, they were asked to comment, in detail, on whether or not the amount of water had changed during the pouring procedure. The answers the young people gave were all videoed.

Although everyone agreed that the quantity of water had not changed, something extremely interesting emerged from observing the taped answers. When the sighted pourers put their descriptions and reasoning into words, they all used gestures such as curving their hands into a 'C' shape to represent grasping the cup, and varying the distance between their hands in order to describe the shapes of the containers.

Amazingly, and to everyone's surprise, the blind people used the same gestures just as often, and in precisely the same way!

This suggested that mimicking was not the sole source of hand movements. The hunt was now on for the real reason, and the next possibility was that we use gestures as an audio-visual aid, in order to give our audience more information and to lend emphasis to our spoken words. To check this theory, the two researchers devised another ingenious experiment on the same lines.

They asked four different blind people to perform exactly the same pouring experiment and to answer the same question. However, this time the person posing the question was blind as well, and the blind pourer knew this.

To everybody's amazement, the videos showed all four blind people continued to gesture in the same way, even though they were fully aware that their gesturing could in no way help convey their messages to their blind listeners.

This suggested a third hypothesis for why we use our hands, which the two researchers set about investigating. This time they asked people to look at a cartoon, and then to describe it while being videoed. One group was asked to describe it with their hands free, the other group while they were sitting on their hands. The results of this experiment showed that when the subjects were later asked to describe the cartoon again, their memories were far clearer if they gesticulated during their original description. What this suggests is that 'waving our hands about' when we speak is a method both of communicating to our listeners *and* of communicating with ourselves!

When you gesture, your body is actually helping your brain to sculpt the words, to clarify the meaning and the message, and to help people think and remember.

Your body is an amazing instrument for expressing your Verbal Intelligence. The eyes, mouth and facial muscles provide infinite combinations of added meanings to your words.

Similarly your torso and its limbs add another gigantic range of additional possibilities for adding bulk to your words.

Finally, your hands, the instruments of genius, allow you to paint infinite pictures and sculpt infinite structures in support of your words.

Case Study – Brain and Body in Sync

Dr Elizabeth Bates, a cognitive scientist from the University of California at San Diego, has found that many imaging studies of the human brain show an overlap between language centres, movement and physical control centres, and other brain regions. She says: 'It makes sense that we find more and more examples of how [these different brain regions] travel together.'

your voice

Your voice emanates from the most amazing and musical instrument ever conceived. A billion-faceted masterpiece which is capable of speaking myriad languages, mimicking any accent, singing wonderful and varied songs, and varying its tone, pitch, energy and projection with incredible finesse.

All of this in support and as part of your Verbal Intelligence!

It is essential, therefore, that you look after this amazing instrument and learn to play it well.

Before that, however, here is an amusing and true story to demonstrate the point.

Can I Sell You a Boat?

In Sweden, an unfortunately shy young man had just started his career as a boat salesman, and was having a singular lack of success. I asked him to show me how he used his Verbal Intelligence in a sales situation, which he proceeded to do.

He explained that there were three kinds of boats he was selling: little boats, medium-sized boats and very big boats (well over 100 metres).

His voice was a monotone, jerky, mumbled, lacking in energy and very quiet.

More interestingly (and amusingly!) his body's support of his words was not just absent, it was contradictory!

When he was describing the small boats, the only gesture he used

---

body talk – body language and how to improve it

was to hold his two hands up and indicate the size, as you would indicate the size of a fish you had caught. The size he demonstrated was about the width of his body. When he described the medium-sized boats, he jerked his two hands up and down for a moment and moved them slightly closer together!

When he came to describe the enormous boats, he once again jerked his hands up and down, and moved them *much* closer together! When he had finished describing the big boats, his hands were almost clasped in prayer!

His Verbal Intelligence score was approaching a negative number!

Your Verbal Intelligence rises with the degree of congruence between your body, voice and words. It sinks, as an uncared-for boat will, if it is disintegrated.

The reason for this disintegration often can be found in the words we use to help us think. These words and images have an immediate impact on your body and voice.

Think of feeling happy, successful and positively directed towards a good goal. With such thoughts your body will improve its poise and posture and therefore its overall presence. With melancholic, depressing and negative thoughts, your body will slump and lose both energy and presence.

A fascinating spiral is created:

When you think well with good and positive words, the instruments that carry your spoken Verbal Intelligence become more energized, alert and ready to give body to the words themselves. When this occurs, your Verbal Intelligence immediately rises. Your audience then also become more energized, and gives you more positive feedback. This increases your energy, improves your poise, ...

To increase your Verbal Intelligence you must integrate positive thinking, physical health, your body language, your multi-talented voice and your words.

Here is another Verbal Workout to help you create this complete Verbal IQ package!

Verbal Workout

Word Puzzle Number 11

1. latzw   __ __ __ __ X
2. fyniot   X X X __ __ X
3. madyon   __ __ X X __ __
4. vibsuoo   __ X __ __ __ X __

Clue: Thinks you're a genius. __ __ __ __   __ __ __ __ __

Verbal Intelligence Tip

- Rest/sleep on it

Why?

Because, as you learned in the first of these Verbal Intelligence Tips in Chapter 1, your brain, as far as solutions to problems is concerned, is a giant incubator. If 'immediate' techniques have not brought the solution to light, allow that giant para-conscious brain of yours to work on it in peace. Don't harass or worry at it – that will simply make your para-conscious retreat; just let it be, and it will work, like the ultimate genie, in your service.

You will all have noticed this phenomenon – when you have taken exams in school, or been asked a tricky question in a job interview, or simply when you needed a quick retort. It is the kind of situation where you *know* you know the answer or phrase you want, but it's not quite in the forefront of your brain – more on the tip of your tongue but not coming off it!

Try as you might to grasp the answer, it is all to no avail. And then, infuriatingly, as you walk out of the examination room or interview, or when the other person is out of earshot, the answer comes flooding back in!

Has it happened to you?! If not you are one-in-a-hundred, because for 99 per cent of the population this is a common occurrence. It happened simply because they did not know how to look after their 'genie'.

You now do!

Word Puzzle Number 12

Circle is to globe as square is to ...?

Study Your Voice

Study and observe your own voice in order to improve its range of skills. Remember – your voice is a musical and Verbal Intelligence instrument; you are the one person who can improve all its qualities.

Check, using audiotape recorders, friends' feedback, your own self-awareness and (where possible) video feedback, the following:

- Your general voice energy level
- Your variation
- Your projection
- Your pitch (high to low)
- Your tone (soft/warm/hard/cold, etc.)
- Your general 'sound quality'.

Rate yourself on a scale of 0-10 on each of these areas, and start the improvement process.

Alternatively, join your local amateur dramatics association – perfect for developing your voice and body-language partnership!

Smile!

Smile at yourself and at others. Research confirms that when you smile at others they will tend to smile back at you. More than this, when you or anyone else smiles, the body releases positive chemicals, and

---

becomes better poised. This leads to a more positive attitude, and therefore a more positive-vocabulary thought process. You can add to this power by 'smiling to yourself', giving yourself a radiance within.

Increasingly, businesses are encouraging their staff to answer phone calls with a smile. It relaxes the person answering the phone, and the caller can also 'hear' the smile, which helps put them into a more positive and cheerful mood! Perfect for customer-complaints departments!

Smile and the world smiles with you!

Smile and your Verbal Intelligence grows!

Check Your Body Language

Check for congruence/incongruence in your own and others' body language and spoken words. Remember the Swedish boat-salesman's story. Remember also that the more fully integrated, healthy, relaxed and honest people are, the more congruent they will be. Their body language will match their verbal language, and their verbal language will match their body language.

Check this in your own conversations and speech. Work towards an increasingly integrated approach in everything you say and do.

Similarly, check for integrated body language in new acquaintances and friends, sales people, public figures, teachers, television broadcasters and (especially!) politicians. Your brain is designed to pick up these cues to help you survive, and *The Power of Verbal Intelligence* will help you to enhance these powers.

One simple way to check your body's super-logical knowledge when you meet a new acquaintance, is to ask yourself:

   (a) 'Do I immediately like this person?' and
   (b) 'Would I trust this person with my most treasured friends and belongings?'

If your answer to either of these questions is 'No', immediately go into your 'Sherlock Holmes Verbal/Body Language detective' mode, and find out the reason why your brain, so rapidly and brilliantly, came to such a conclusion.

As well as providing you with essential information for your continued security, success and happiness, this study will provide you with endless hours of entertainment and amusement!

Mirror Exercises

Stand in front of a full-length mirror and chat to yourself! There is *not* more to this exercise than 'meets the eye'. There is *exactly* as much as meets the eye! For here, while chatting away to yourself, you will be examining every move you make, position your body takes, and expression your eyes and face make, while you speak.

At first you may find doing this a bit embarrassing or intimidating, but it will rapidly become fun and useful – you are, after all, chatting with a friend who has been your companion and supporter throughout your life!

Keep a record of every strength and weakness you observe. Then use the strengths to improve on the weaknesses. That 'mirror on the wall' will let you know about your progress in your vocabulary and presentation skills, helping you toward your goal of becoming 'the fairest of them all'!

Play Vocal Games

Experiment and play games with your voice. This Workout involves both your body and your ability to behave and learn like the ultimate vocabulary acquirer – the child. At least once a day, perhaps in the shower or your car (don't you often see people singing/chatting to themselves as they drive by you?!), experiment with different vocal sounds, volumes and variations. This is like doing physical stretching exercises for your body – it expands both the width and strength of the instrument. It is also fun to do.

Children often play these sorts of games, and if you can join in with them, do!

Sing!

Sing – either privately or publicly! Singing will give you similar benefits to the exercise above, but in a more structurally creative way. When a tune 'lodges' in your head, let it free; when you are encouraged to join in at the local karaoke bar, do so; when you are feeling happy or sad, sing songs to yourself; whenever the spirit moves you, allow your musical soul to express itself. As you now know, this release of your musical energy will only benefit and increase the power of your Verbal Intelligence.

Check Your Vocabulary's Positive/Negative Ratio

Check your private and public vocabularies for their positive/negative ratio. If either or both of them is filled with negatives, remind yourself that this reduces your physical energy, weakens your immune system, pulls down your posture and poise, increases your probability of failure, de-motivates you, *and does the same for those around you*!

Resolve to fill the new reservoirs of your Verbal Intelligence with more positive, energetic and life-enhancing travelling companions.

Word Power Booster Number 6

In this Word Booster I am going to introduce you to words about words, to further enrich your knowledge of the study in which you are now engaged. Choose the definition that you think is closest to the correct meaning from the four options given for each word.

1 CLICHÉ (*klée*-shay)

    (a) Private meaning

    (b) Secret area

    (c) Hackneyed or stereotyped phrase

    (d) Witty pun

2 SIMILE (*sím*-illee)

    (a) Radiant expression

    (b) Comparing one thing with another

    (c) Long expression

    (d) Contradiction

3 AMBIGUITY (am-big-*yú*-i-tee)
- (a) Quite big
- (b) Large meaning
- (c) Unclear
- (d) Eloquently expressed

4 EUPHEMISM (*yú*-fa-mism)
- (a) An untruth
- (b) A mild word substituted for one that is more direct
- (c) A word evoking the sense of smell
- (d) A beautiful sounding word

5 NON SEQUITUR (non *sék*-wi-ter)
- (a) A conclusion that does not follow from the facts
- (b) Out of order
- (c) A dress without sequins
- (d) Not resigning in sequence

6 REDUNDANCY (re-*dún*-dan-see)
- (a) Stupid
- (b) Unnecessary repetition; no longer needed
- (c) An over abundance of the colour crimson
- (d) Worthless

7 EPIGRAM (*ép*-e-gram)

    (a) Twice the weight of a gram

    (b) Half the weight of a gram

    (c) A concise and witty saying

    (d) A Latin law of grammar

8 ONOMATOPOEIA (ono-*mátt*a-peer)

    (a) Boring sound

    (b) Single sound

    (c) A word that sounds like what it describes

    (d) A word that does not sound like what it describes

9 PERSIFLAGE (*pérsy*-flage)

    (a) Light mockery or banter

    (b) Flowery speech

    (c) Description of flowers

    (d) Closed shoot

10 METAPHOR (*mét*-a-for)

    (a) A greeting

    (b) Something implying a resemblance to something else

    (c) A gas which causes drowsiness

    (d) A type of bacteria

present yourself –

how to become a successful speaker

chapter seven

'A word fitly spoken is like apples of gold in pitchers of silver.'

Proverbs 25:11

'Whose words all ears took captive.'

Shakespeare

Making presentations gives you the ultimate opportunity to express yourself and to let your Verbal Intelligence bloom.

Yet, surprisingly, making presentations and speaking in public is the Number 1 fear on the planet!

Why?

Because lack of confidence in your Verbal Intelligence, and the high probability that speaking in public will expose your perceived low Verbal IQ, is a very valid reason for feeling afraid.

In this chapter I will introduce you to information and exercises that will help you on your path to becoming an excellent speaker.

You will be able to combine what you have learned from previous chapters with the new information here to help you become a powerful and entertaining speaker.

Case Study – Hold Your Tongue!

It is obviously good to be able to know how and when to speak. It is also good to know when not to!

Cardiologists have known for some time that blood pressure can rise in the doctor's surgery. But why? Claude Le Pailleur and his colleagues at the Necker Hospital wanted to know more about the factors involved.

They devised an experiment in which they compared blood-pressure readings taken while volunteers were sitting in the doctor's surgery doing nothing, with those taken from patients who were either talking or reading a book.

The readings reduced slightly for those reading a book compared with those doing nothing. The blood pressure of those who talked rose sharply!

The researchers suggest that if you chat enthusiastically with your doctor during a check-up, you could be prescribed drugs you don't need.

Use your newly developing speaking skills *after* your blood pressure has been taken!

the speaking situation

When you are faced with giving a presentation at work, or any other situation where you have to give a speech in front of other people, the first thing to do is to think about the situation you are *really* in. You are a Verbally Intelligent person who has the goal of using that Intelligence to express yourself to other Verbally Intelligent people!

As you express yourself to them, your sub-goals will be:

- To entertain them as you speak.
- To have them understand clearly what you say.
- To have them remember what you convey.
- To facilitate their use of what you say.
- To captivate them by your words.
- To make a good and lasting impression.

'Speech is power: speech is to persuade, to convert, to compel.'

Ralph Waldo Emerson

Hooked on Words

One of the most brilliant boxers ever to emerge from the British Isles was Irishman Barry McGuigan. McGuigan rapidly rose up in the boxing ranks and became the World Featherweight Champion in 1985. He was renowned for his exquisite boxing skills, and was described as the perfect practitioner of the 'sweet science'. In addition, he was renowned for his positive attitude, his ability to take any set-back in his stride and to learn from it, and for his total dedication to his training.

After he had retired McGuigan became one of the top elite boxers elected to the prestigious Boxing Hall of Fame, an honour reserved for the very few who are considered by the sporting community to be among the greatest champions, as well as individuals who are great ambassadors for their sport.

As soon as he retired, McGuigan was eagerly approached by TV companies to become a specialized boxing commentator, which he did.

When he began his new career, McGuigan became very aware that his commentating style was in the order of the following: 'and that was a terrific left jab thrown by Jones followed by a terrific right cross …and Smith comes back with a terrific right uppercut and a terrific left jab …'. He decided to improve his Verbal Intelligence!

McGuigan literally 'went into training' to improve his Verbal IQ, using all the training techniques he had learned as a world-champion athlete. To aid him he used Mind Maps to help him expand his vocabulary, and his increasing knowledge of the wonder of words.

Within a short time his vocabulary and Verbal Intelligence improved dramatically. Rather than 'terrific … terrific … terrific …' McGuigan began to spice up his commentary with 'lightning-like, stunning, juddering, rapier-fast, jolting, electrifying …'. Having applied the training techniques he had used to become a world-champion physical athlete, he rapidly rose up the ranks of TV sports commentators, and became a champion in the *mental* sphere!

McGuigan was so impressed with the rapid strides he was able to make in the development of his Verbal Intelligence that he now plays Verbal Intelligence games with his children – using Mind Maps® and memory techniques to help them as Mind Maps® helped him.

You can achieve the same results as he did!

your audience

Think carefully about your audience. Their brains and Verbal Intelligences operate identically to yours.

Therefore you know that they operate on the basis of the multi-ordinate nature of words, and that their brains form gigantic networks and maps of associations, before, during and after you speak to them.

You know that they will understand and remember more at the beginnings and ends of your presentation. You know especially that they will understand and remember anything that appeals to their imagination and senses, and anything that helps them make links and associations. You know that one of the best ways to do all this is to tell stories, for stories appeal to all the elements of our memory and creativity.

You also know that you have the knowledge to help them understand and remember, link and associate. You also know that you have an increasingly rich and varied vocabulary, a voice which is unparalleled in its ability to convey information to them, and a body which, when allowed to express itself in congruence with your words, content and voice, adds enormous power to your message.

In addition to all this, your body has its five magical senses to add to the formula, which enhance, on all levels, your ability to present information and your own Verbal Intelligence.

'How forceful are right words.'

Job 6:25

What the following Workout is focused upon is the idea that in order to be a superb presenter and to manifest your genius of Verbal Intelligence, all you have to do is to *Be Yourself!*

The Workout will help you on that path ...

verbal workout

Word Puzzle Number 13

1. venet   _ _ X X X
2. dioua   _ X _ _ X
3. bidlee   _ _ _ _ X X
4. veriuq   X _ _ _ _ _

Clue: After becoming a graduate of *The Power of Verbal Intelligence* you will be:

_ _ _ _ _ _ _ _

Verbal Intelligence Tip

- Look for Prefixes, Suffixes and Roots.

Why?

You know! Let me expand further: Prefixes, Suffixes and Roots make up a large percentage of the total number of letters found in the total number of words. As a result, if you look for them when you are trying to unscramble a scrambled word, you have a higher probability of being successful in your search than if you just 'go random'. The new word-friends you have made in Chapters 3 and 4 will be of great assistance to you here, and will help you to raise your Verbal IQ even more.

Word Puzzle Number 14

The brain and behaviour is to psychology, as mind and body are to ... ?

Shout It Out!

Case Study – Speak Up

There is now proof from the neuro-biological laboratories that the volume of confidence with which you speak does affect the brains of those listening. The main body of each neuron (the brain cell's mini-brain) receives thousands of messages from the junctions (synapses), where the cell's tentacle-like extensions come in contact with other neurons.

These message signals become progressively weaker the further they travel from brain cell to brain cell. How, then, can impulses that travel great distances possibly compete with ones from nearby?

Geoffrey McGee, at the Louisiana State University Medical Center in New Orleans, decided to investigate. He measured the strength of messages at various points along the branches of neurons. He discovered a truth that seems surprisingly obvious when you know it, and which has very significant implications and applications. The stronger the impulse (i.e. the louder the voice) at source, the stronger the signal is when it starts out, and the stronger it is further on down the line.

This means that if you wish to have what you say register in the mind of your audience, you must speak up, be clear, and trigger good and strong associations in your audience.

If you do not, your messages will be lost among the cacophony of competing and stronger sounds.

You obviously need to apply the principles behind Professor McGee's findings whenever you are giving any sort of speech.

There is, however, a much more subtle and very important application of McGee's research – to your own learning. When you are reviewing and revising what you have learned, especially in areas such as vocabulary and language learning, make sure you repeat things *aloud*. In this way you will be reinforcing your own brain with the strength of the signal you are sending to it.

If you are reviewing silently, for example in a library, don't silently whisper, silently SHOUT! If you imagine the loud sound, the response in your brain will be the same as if you had actually heard it. In any library you can shout as loudly as you like – as long as you do it silently!

Tell Stories

Listen to story-tellers; *become* a storyteller! When you develop your ability to become a mesmerizing storyteller, you are well over half way on your journey to becoming a superb speaker. From now on, when you are in the presence of good storytellers, use the technique of mimicking that babies use so effectively to help you become as skilled as them.

Study in detail the elements of their own mastery, especially their vocabulary, imagination and body language.

Review your own life for 'amazing stories' from your own past. Choose those that are the most exciting, most ridiculous, most informative, most extraordinary, most hair-raising, most absurd and most tantalizing! Practise re-telling them to close friends, and polish them up to the level where they can be presented successfully in any situation.

In the same way, listen out for superb stories from your family and friends, and put them into your own 'story bag'.

Learn to Project Your Voice

It is not natural for our voices to be kept in a medium range. The only reason they are is social, and can be traced back to our school days, where we were continually told to 'be quiet', or to social situations where it was considered impolite to raise your voice. Your voice naturally wants to experiment with its full range of volumes, especially loud! Sensibly, society has arranged certain events and activities in which it is not only permitted to raise your voice; you are actually encouraged to do so.

The growing popularity of karaoke nights provides excellent opportunities to give your voice the workout it so desperately needs! Next time you get the chance, go along to one. If you don't get the opportunity, make one!

Another type of event where you are positively encouraged to make a noise is in the football ground, or at other sporting venues. There you are expected to chant, sing, cheer and shout. Encourage yourself to go to these as often as you can, and give your voice a real high-powered workout.

Another area where the loud use of your voice is generally accepted is walking the dog. I am convinced that one of the main reasons people enjoy walking their dogs is not only for the fresh air, but for the opportunity to yell their heads off in nature's wide open spaces! They can shout and bellow commands at their (usually oblivious) dogs to their heart's content!

Practice Accents and Different Pronunciations

As you must be realizing more and more, your voice is an astonishingly flexible and trainable instrument. If you had been born anywhere in the world where one of the world's 2,000 languages was spoken rather than your own, you would have learnt it. You still can. Learning different local and international accents gives your voice more range, while adding considerably to your ability to understand and entertain others.

Use Word Pictures

When you use word pictures you are combining the skills of your left and right brain hemispheres: words from the left and images/imagination from the right. By combining them, you create a multiplier effect in the power of your words.

Just think, for example, of simply reciting the sentence 'I really enjoyed eating that big bowl of fruit.'

Now imagine that it was a hot summer day, you had not eaten for four days, and suddenly the most delicious bowl of fruit you had ever seen was placed in front of you. Every piece of fruit was perfectly ripe, beautifully coloured and giving off the most tempting and delicious aroma. Even more, the bowl contained every one of your own personal favourites. Imagine that you devoured it ravenously, and that it was the most gorgeous and memorable meal that you had ever had.

Now imagine saying that original sentence again, this time with full memory and full passion.

This technique, combining words with powerful, sensual images, is what all the great poets and writers, especially Shakespeare, use with such great success. When you use the technique, it will help to raise *your* Verbal Intelligence too.

Check Your Own Self-Talk

As well as checking the conversations you have with and the speeches you make to others, check the conversations you have and the speeches you make to *yourself*. Many people are wonderful conversationalists and public speakers; at the same time they often save all their worst, most depressing, negative and demotivating speeches for themselves! They are constantly telling themselves they can't do things: that they're 'no good', that they'll 'never succeed'. This is the worse kind of speaking/coaching!

If you notice any such tendency in yourself, including torrents of negative word use when you fail or mess things up, analyse why, put that type of demotivating vocabulary back on the shelf where it belongs, give yourself a pat on the back, and start to be a much better conversationalist with yourself!

Energize Your Voice – Improve Your Memory

Your memory works better when things are emphasized, imaginative and outstanding. If you are one of those people who constantly forgets because you have scribbled things you wanted to remember on lost scraps of paper, or repeated such things silently in a monotonous and uninspired voice, use this much better technique: whatever you want to remember, repeat it to yourself with *added extra energy*.

When you do this, your brain will feel more positive towards whatever it is you repeated, simply because of the extra energy with which you have said it. Additionally, the extra energy will make the statement 'stand out' in your mind's eye, and when things stand out, your brain remembers much more easily.

Establish Your Personal Presentation Goals

Complete a mini Mind Map® of the areas in which you specifically want to improve your speaking skills. Areas to consider should include:

- One-on-one conversations with family and/or friends and colleagues
- Joke-telling
- Storytelling
- Informal presentations on a particular subject to small groups/teams
- Giving instructions/directions
- Special-occasion speeches, such as Best Man and After-dinner speeches
- Professional presentations to large groups.

When you have established these goals, quickly re-read the chapter, and start to apply these Verbal Workout suggestions to help achieve them.

Case Study – Think First!

Think about what you are going to say before you actually say it. If you do you will be at a considerable advantage.

That's the finding from a study on stuttering by researchers in Finland and Germany. Riitta Salmenlin and her colleagues at the Helsinki University of Technology asked 9 long-term stutterers and 10 fluent speakers to read out individual words from a list. As they read, their brain activity was monitored by devices which identify precisely where and, crucially, when, certain regions of the brain are being activated.

The fluent speakers first activated a part of the brain that decides what to say and then, afterwards, a part that works out exactly how to say it. The stutterers' brains did exactly the opposite. 'Stutterers were somehow initiating their mouth muscles before they knew what they were going to say,' said Salmenlin.

All of us have, in varying degrees, experienced this 'Stutterers' Syndrome' where our mouth gets into gear before our brain and what comes out is jumbled, incorrect or incomprehensible!

Brain research now confirms that a little thought given to preparation (and Mind Maps are particularly useful in this instance) will make your message much clearer, and you more Verbally Intelligent – and intelligible!

Word Power Booster Number 7

Now that you have learnt more about the relationship of Verbal Intelligence to speaking, you will appreciate especially the following 10 words, which will allow you to wax lyrical about speaking with even more erudition!

Each word contains the Root 'loqui' or 'loc', from the Latin '*loquor*', '*locutus*', meaning speech. Choose the definition you think is closest to the correct meaning.

1 ELOQUENCE (*elló*-kwence)
   (a) Elongated speech
   (b) Musical speech
   (c) Speech full of power and imagination
   (d) Low-level speech

2 ELOCUTION (ello-*cué*-shon)
   (a) Elongated speech
   (b) Strict education
   (c) Single 'cutting' conversation
   (d) Clear and expressive speech

3 LOQUACIOUS (lo-*kwáy*-shus)
   (a) Speech from a specific area
   (b) Talkative; garrulous
   (c) Rhythmical speech
   (d) Wave-like rhythms in speech

4 SOLILOQUY (so-*lill*-o-kwee)
   (a) Talking about the sun
   (b) Talking about being alone
   (c) Speaking thoughts aloud when alone; monologue
   (d) Speech given near boats

5 CIRCUMLOCUTION (sercum-lo-*cúe*-shun)
   (a) Discussion of the geometry of circles
   (b) Using many words where one will do
   (c) Discussion of circumcision
   (d) Medical term for stuttering

6 INTERLOCUTION (inter-lo-*cúe*-shun)
   (a) Interruption
   (b) Illogical interjection
   (c) To talk around
   (d) Conversation; exchange of speech

7 LOQUENT (*ló*-kwent)
   (a) Silent; disinclined to speak
   (b) Articulate; inclined to speak
   (c) Waiting to speak
   (d) Unable to speak

8 INTERLOCUTRESS (inter-*lóc*-uetress)

(a) A female interlocutor

(b) Discussion about hair

(c) Actress who speaks

(d) Cute female speaker

9 LOCUTION (lo-*cúe*-shun)

(a) A lesson in good speech

(b) 'Beating about the bush'

(c) Shortened version of 'elocution'

(d) A person's style of speech

10 ELOCUTE (*éllo*-cute)

(a) Witty speech

(d) To pronounce well

(c) To declaim; to speak out in public

(d) To use bad language in a high-sounding manner

chapter eight

'Newspapers, magazines and TV and computer screens are some of your windows on the world and, increasingly, the universe. It is possible, by understanding their nature, and some new approaches to them, to increase your efficiency in this area by a factor of ten.'

Tony Buzan

One of the best ways to improve your Verbal Intelligence is to learn to get rapid control and command of the words that confront you – especially in books, magazines and newspapers – to learn how to absorb them with speed and with understanding, and to be able to recall them when you need to.

This chapter will help you do just that, as well as introducing you to your amazing Cyclopean Magic Eye.

getting control of all those words

One of the greatest stumbling blocks to the development of Verbal Intelligence is the inability to study academic, professional or 'hard' materials properly.

A person with a low Verbal Intelligence will attack these situations head on, attempting to read the book from beginning to end, reading one or two words at a time, reading slowly and carefully for better comprehension, always reading page 5 before page 6, never looking at the end of the book until they have fought their way through to it, and taking written notes as they do.

A person with a powerful Verbal Intelligence does exactly the opposite!

A high Verbal IQ knows that the way to master words and information is first to get an overview of the entire work, checking such things as Tables of Contents, indices, chapter headings, sub-headings, illustrations, photographs and graphs, introductions and, especially, summaries.

Why?

Because this Verbally smart behaviour roots out all the *key words*, *ideas* and *images*, and gives the reader an immediate and overall picture and grasp of the subject at hand.

What's more, rather than taking linear and inappropriate written notes, the Verbally Intelligent person will take Mind Map® notes that help reflect the network of the information being studied.

reading faster

One of the great mistakes made by people whose Verbal Intelligence is still fairly low, is to assume that their brains will operate better, and understand and comprehend more, if they read one word at a time, slowly and carefully.

Once again, although this sounds logical it is exactly the opposite of what is necessary.

The eye/brain system does not and cannot operate in this way.

To grasp this concept clearly, imagine someone speaking to you slowly, carefully, methodically and monotonously, one word at a time! You would find them incomprehensible, utterly forgettable, and unbelievably boring!

Why allow the pages in front of you to speak to you in the same way?

Think about how your brain understands words best: when they are spoken to you in a comfortably fast, properly phrased and rhythmical manner.

So it must be with a book. Allow your eyes to travel faster along the page than they usually do. Take in meaningful phrases rather than words. Maintain a comfortable rhythm.

To add to your speed, use a guide pointer, such as a thin pen or pencil or a chopstick. Move this pace-fully along, much as you do when you use a finger or pencil to glide down margins of a dictionary or telephone directory when you are looking for a word or a number.

This gives focus, relaxes the eyes, improves concentration and accelerates the speed.

cyclopean perception – your magic eye

In the middle of the 20th century, a pioneering visual researcher by the name of Bella Julesz made an astonishing discovery: that we have a 'Third Eye'. Julesz designed pictures that looked like normal colourful squiggly patterns. When looked at with normal vision they stayed the same. When looked at with the left eye only, they stayed the same. When looked at with the right eye only, they stayed the same.

When looked at out of focus, and with both eyes, an amazing thing happened. The brain took the two separate images from the left and right eyes, and placed them over each other. As they 'clicked into place' a third, three-dimensional holographic image suddenly leapt from the page.

Julesz called it 'Cyclopean Perception', after the mythical giant Cyclops, who had only one eye.

The fact that the eye/brain system can do this magical perception feat shows that the brain is taking in 'the whole picture' no matter what it is looking at.

The Verbally Intelligent person, being aware of this, keeps a more wide-open eye and a bigger perception when reading, not only words, but the entire environment.

There are other ways to improve the background forces that support your reading, and these are explored in the Verbal Workout later.

remembering what you have read

You are already using the technique! Once again the Mind Map®
comes to your rescue.

The Verbally Intelligent person, rather than taking standard,
forgettable linear notes, will Mind Map® the material as he or she
speeds along, building up an associative map of words and images
that reflect the content of the material read, and the reader's growing
understanding of it.

Thanks to its pictorial, verbal and associative nature, the Mind
Map® acts as a perfect memory tool.

verbal workout

Word Puzzle Number 15

1. nunyf   __ X __ __ X
2. yagvoe   X __ __ X __ __
3. lobime   __ X X __ X __
4. catryof   __ X X __ __ X __

Clue: Phenomenal brain tool.

__ __ __ __ __ __ __ __ __ __

Verbal Intelligence Tip

■ Look for standard patterns of 'letter and word behaviour'.

Why?

Your brain is a pattern-seeking machine, and the more opportunities you can give it to find those patterns, the better. Here are some hints:

1. You know from Chapters 3 and 4 that there are common Prefixes, Suffixes and Roots. Look for these in your scrambled words, and you will find you are often left with only a few remaining letters to fit into the jig-saw, making the whole process much easier.

2. Common endings to look for include: 'ed', 'er', 'ise/ize' and 'y'. If 'y' is amongst your scrambled letters, there is a 90 per cent chance that it will fit at the end of the word.

3. 'q' and 'u'. If these appear in your scrambled letters, there is virtually a 100 per cent certainty that the 'u' will follow immediately after the 'q', so already the pattern of your missing word will be becoming clear.

4. 'o' and 'u'. If these two letters appear in your scrambled word, there is a very strong chance that they will appear together in the form 'ou'.

5. Groupings. By the sheer nature of chance, very often the scrambled word will have been either simply reversed, or its syllables maintained and simply put in a different order. Look for these first, because if this has occurred you can get the answer immediately.

Word Puzzle Number 16

Insert the word that means the same as the two words outside the brackets.

CARD GAME (__ __ __ __ __) ROD

Become a Word Hunter

Now that you have so much more knowledge about the power of words and your own Verbal Intelligence, refine your detective skills, and be on the active lookout for new words that can add power and vivacity to your growing vocabulary.

Wherever possible when you come across new words, highlight, underline, box and star them, to make them stand out in your mind's eye. The simple act of deciding you are going to 'up the ante' will guarantee that you will track down more words, and will capture them better once you have them more powerfully focused in your sights.

Create a 'New Words' Diary

Now that you have progressed so far, it is time to gather up and organize the bounty of treasure you have been collecting. Create a special 'New Words' Diary designed for your maximum benefit. You may wish to keep your new words in the chronological order in which you discovered them; you may wish to keep them in classifications such as nouns, verbs, adjectives etc.; you may wish to keep them in the context of where they were found (long novels, poems, texts, etc.).

Whatever particular method you select, make sure that you 'get your words in order'!

Build a Verbal Intelligence Knowledge File

This Knowledge File is where you collect your 'word treasures'. It will act as your personal Verbal IQ Library, containing all the best word knowledge you have come in contact with in your life.

Sections of your Knowledge File can include:

- Summaries of the best novels you have read
- Favourite poems
- Favourite quotations
- Part or all of your 'New Words' Diary
- Some of the Mind Maps® you have made, which best demonstrate your Verbal Intelligence
- Jokes which play on the meanings of words and which you think are especially funny.

Use the Index

Whenever you are reading a book that contains an Index, make sure that one of the first things you do is to scan through it. This is a habit common to all people with high Verbal Intelligence.

Why?

Because the Index can be a superb keyword summary of all the main concepts and ideas within the book. It acts like a magic key that unlocks the secret of the contents.

All the words from the Index, once registered in your brain, will act like hundreds of special hooks that will latch on to all the information within the book as you read it. They will make your reading easier, more meaningful, more memorable and faster.

Make Your Reading Environment a Playground For Words

Many people make their study look and feel much like a prison cell! They have a bare table, stark chair, blank, single-tone walls, no music, no art and often inadequate lighting and little fresh air. Why do they do this? Because in their minds the idea of 'study' has come to mean drudgery, boredom, examinations, stress, forgetting, detentions, punishment, failure, slavery and prison!

It need not, indeed it *should not*, be this way!

Your study should be a playground for words. It should be somewhere your brain loves, and cannot wait to be in. As you already know, music and song stimulate Verbal Intelligence, so have music and song in your verbal playground. Your verbal playground should be inviting, comfortable, colourful, stimulating, brightly lit (ideally with daylight) and with freshly circulating air – and *filled* with dictionaries, Thesauruses, encyclopaedias, your special favourite and treasured books, and whatever electronic media you think will inspire you in the exploration and growth of your Verbal Intelligence.

Reward yourself. Entice yourself. Treat your Verbal Intelligence to all the things which inspire it and which it loves. Give that eternal verbal child in you the playground for which it has always longed.

Commit Yourself to Your Verbal Intelligence

Commit to lifelong learning and the development of your Verbal Intelligence. Every year commit to learn at least one new Root, one new Prefix and one new Suffix. Then commit to learn at least 10 words that contain these. This will give you at least 30 new words per year, and more: it will give you new 'energy centres', each one of which will itself be self-perpetuating, making more associations, connecting with your rapidly growing vocabulary, and helping you, naturally and easily, to latch on to even more new words and concepts.

This simple and easy programme will allow you, over your lifetime, to more than quadruple your vocabulary.

Play With Your 'Magic Eye'

At least once a month, play with your Cyclopean perception. Invest in a book of Magic Eye images, and have fun going in and out of focus with the images. This will keep your 'big vision' well exercised, and will automatically enable you to see more in your normal reading, and so maintain your higher reading speeds and better comprehension.

Word Power Booster Number 8

In this Word Booster we are going 'back to your Roots'. Bring all your Verbal Intelligence detective skills to the fore – each of the words you are about to encounter you can dissect, analyse and put back together, confident that you have discovered its meaning. Again, choose the definition you think is closest to the correct meaning from the options given.

---

1 PHILANTHROPY (fill-*án*-thropee)

   (a) Love of mankind

   (b) Hatred of mankind

   (c) Fear of mankind

   (d) Wasting energy

2 MONOTHEISM (mono-*thée*-isum)

   (a) Belief that religion is boring

   (b) Belief in a specific religion

   (c) Belief in a single supreme deity

   (d) Meditation on the nature of God

3 MISANTHROPY (mis-*ánth*-ropee)

   (a) Love of mankind

   (b) Hatred of mankind

   (c) Study of the female human

   (d) Confusion about mankind

4 PHILOLOGY (fill-*ól*-ogee)

   (a) The study of philosophy

   (b) The love of philosophy

   (c) The love of words and the study of language

   (d) Aversion to knowledge

5 HOLANTHROPY (holl-*án*-thropee)
  (a) The study of the whole human being
  (b) Gaps in knowledge about mankind
  (c) Studying the overview of human history
  (d) Synonym for misanthropy

6 MONOGAMY (monóg-amee)
  (a) Monotonous speech
  (b) Practice of being married to one person at a time
  (c) Neat handwriting; fine script
  (d) Depression about relationships

7 BICUSPID (*bí*-cuspid)
  (a) An animal descended from two evolutionary branches
  (b) An animal with two large-pronged teeth
  (c) A tooth with two prongs
  (d) A form of bicycle

8 ANTHROPOLOGY (anthro-*pól*-ogee)
  (a) The study of coals
  (b) The study of human history and development
  (c) Apologist for mankind
  (d) Disdain for mankind

9 PHILLUMENIST (fill-*lú*-menist)

    (a) A pyromaniac

    (b) A lover of light

    (c) A collector of matchboxes

    (d) A lover of knowledge

10 POLYGLOT (*pólli*-glot)

    (a) One stuffs himself with food

    (b) A chatterbox

    (c) Lover of languages

    (d) One who speaks many languages

chapter nine

'Words are the dress of thoughts.'

Chesterfield

'Words are the most powerful drug used by mankind.'

Kipling

The bulk of this chapter will be given over to an extensive Verbal Workout, in which I will show you ways of making communication more memorable, and using all the knowledge you have gained so far to enhance your Verbal Intelligence in all forms of communication.

First, though, a story, and a few main topics for you to consider, including the multi-ordinate nature of words, once again, the giving of directions and the secrets behind animal communications.

the multi-ordinate nature of words revisited

In a classroom for 5-year olds, the teacher asked the children to draw a picture from the Lord's Prayer.

Most children drew pictures of heaven, clouds, angels, a loaf of bread, a king's crown, etc.

One little girl, however, drew something quite different and, at first glance, indecipherable. She drew a big circle with two little protrusions at the bottom, and next to is a much, much smaller circle, similarly with two protrusions at the bottom.

After the teacher had marked the assignment, she came back to the classroom and distributed the pictures, generally with high praise for the artists. When she came to the two circles, however, she turned to the child and said: 'I asked you to draw a picture from the Lord's Prayer – this is not what I asked you for.'

Eventually, to the teacher's mortified embarrassment, the little girl's explanation of what she had drawn indicated that it certainly *was* a picture from the Lord's Prayer.

It was a picture of God leading us not into temptation!

Illustration depicting a child's drawing of The Lord's Prayer.

the power of verbal intelligence

This story indicates just how important it is, in all forms of communication, to realize the internal Mind Maps® that exist in the minds of those who receive your communications.

The task facing the Verbally Intelligent with the multi-ordinate nature of words is neatly summed up in this witty statement: *'I know that you believe that you understand what you think I said, but I am not sure you realize that what you heard is not what I meant!'*

This is particularly true in the giving of directions.

directions

Most people who give directions give them only with consideration to the pictures and structures they have in their own minds. Most people who receive such instructions get lost.

Directions often take the form of the following:

'To get where you want to go, go down this road a little while, turn left at the pub, go along for a little way further, turn right by the petrol station – now let me see, was it BP, Esso, Shell ... I can't quite remember, sorry, anyway, when you turn, carry on down the road until you see a field with horses in it. After that turn left and the place you want is just down the road.'

No wonder people get lost!

The reason for this vagueness is that the person has not yet developed his or her Verbal IQ; he or she has a very clear picture of the appropriate route, but is not yet Verbally Intelligent enough to convey it to another.

The things that are missing are the very things that are essential to a Verbally Intelligent transaction:

- Distance. Distance is essential for the brain, it allows the right brain-spatial skills to 'click in' and help solve the problem.
- Clear, imaginative descriptions of the major landmark images (buildings etc.) on the route. These need to be visually outstanding and different from the rest of the environment.
- Time to be taken. Giving the time gives the receiving brain a cross-check on distance.

A Verbally Intelligent version of the directions given above might go something like this:

'Go down this road for about a mile, and you'll come to an old black-and-white beamed pub on the corner. Turn left there and go along that road for another half-mile or so, and you will see a whopping great petrol station. Take the right turn immediately after the petrol station, and go past some low white buildings, which look a bit like a long row of matchboxes. Keep on that road for a couple of miles and then you will see a gently rising field with stockade fencing and some horses. Take the next left turn after that field, and the place you want is about 100 yards down the road. It shouldn't take you longer than 10–15 minutes to drive.'

This far clearer set of directions, accurate as it may well be, will always be checked by the Verbally Intelligent. Why? Because the Verbally Intelligent know that the receiver's brain may well 'create' false data on the basis of what has been said.

Giving clear, concise, visual, descriptive and accurate directions is an infallible sign of a person with a high Verbal Intelligence. If they are capable of accomplishing such a feat, this individual will inevitably be successful in all other forms of communication.

It is interesting to note that giving good directions involves using imagination and association, as well as accurate location. This is exactly what a Mind Map® does, as a tool for giving clear and accurate directions to you as you travel the highways and byways of your growing knowledge.

animal communication

As little as 50 years ago it was thought that animals were fundamentally dumb, and that everything they did was an automatic stimulus-response and not real communication at all.

We now know this to be completely untrue.

Dolphins, whales, the apes, all mammals and birds have incredibly sophisticated and complex communication systems. Interestingly, much of this is done with voice and their 'words'. The rest of their communication is done through their senses and through their body language.

We now know that the sum form of animal-social interaction is almost unbelievably advanced. We now know also that their social structures are highly complex and exceptionally successful.

Animal hunting packs, for example, are often more streamlined than a military unit. Pods of whales have an intricate social structure, and can communicate with those from their pods speaking the same language over distances of hundreds of miles.

What is the relevance of all this to the development of your own Verbal Intelligence?

Simply that by studying the Verbal, Sensual, Vocal and Body Language Intelligence of animals, we can discover many ideas and actions that will enhance our own Verbally Intelligent communications.

Case Study - IQ Speak

Dr Robert Gifford and Dr D'Arcy Reynolds, whose experiment on judging intelligence was covered in Chapter 3 (see page 73), report additional findings that are particularly relevant to understanding *listening*.

It was found that people formed a more accurate and precise opinion of others' intelligence levels by ignoring visual cues. The judges who watched video-tapes of the subjects' talking were relatively unsuccessful in guessing the subjects' true IQ level. However, the judges who listened only to the interviews, without having any sight of the subject on video, had a notably higher success rate.

Knowing that people rate your intelligence more accurately when they only hear you raises an interesting point. If, for example, you wish to impress someone with your Verbal Intelligence, especially in situations such as job interviews, you might try to ensure that your first contact is by telephone.

You will now be able to apply your knowledge of Verbal Intelligence and Communication in your next Verbal Workout.

verbal workout

Word Puzzle Number 17

miper	X X X __ X
arope	X __ __ X X
robew	X __ X __ __
thingk	__ X __ __ __ __

Clue: As you are reading *The Power of Verbal Intelligence* you are developing your:

__ __ __ __ __   __ __ __ __ __

Verbal Intelligence Tip

- Rearrange the letters in a circular pattern

Rearrange the letters into a circle, with vowels generally near the centre and letters that will probably end up near to each other arranged so that their pattern is clearly visible.

For example if we take the word 'catryof' from Word Puzzle Number 15, and lay it out:

The possibility of making connections between the letters is much greater than if we leave them in a line. This allows the phenomenal associative power of your brain to find the possible good connections much more rapidly.

If your first rearrangement isn't successful (and it usually is!), quickly rearrange them again – the second time is nearly always successful.

This is an amazingly useful technique for solving crossword anagrams!

Word Puzzle Number 18

Insert the word that completes the first word and begins the second.

INDIVI (__ __ __ __) ISM

Use Your Memory to Communicate

Remember to apply your knowledge of memory to the art of communication! Among the main principles you have learnt about your memory are that it remembers more of the beginnings; more of the ends; things which are associated; things which are imaginative/outstanding; finally, it remembers much better if review is practised, especially when that review is properly spaced.

When you are communicating, what is your prime goal? To have people understand and *remember* what it is you have said. To enable them to do this, you simply have to apply what you know:

- Make sure that your communications start off with a bang – give them the key elements of what you are going to say, because they will remember these more easily.
- End with a bang! Leave them on a 'high', because the Verbally Intelligent person –you– knows that they will remember the ends best.
- Make sure you link your words and concepts both to each other, and to the people with whom you are communicating. This will enable them to remember the material better, and to make the most important memory link of all: the connection of what you have said to their own personal and professional lives.
- Expand your own communication skills by using your giant imagination to give your words even more meaning. This will make them more memorable in the minds of the audience (and you more memorable as well!) and once again will enable them to remember what you said (and you!) much more easily.

- If you are communicating in a situation which spans days, weeks, months or years, make sure you review for your audience as close to the one hour/one day/one week/one month/six months/long-term memory ideal pacing as you can. This will involve you in far less work, for you will not continuingly be having to drag back forgotten material from the Great Forgettary! And neither will they.

Use the Multi-ordinate Nature of Words

Use the multi-ordinate nature of words as a beacon in all your communication. Knowing that every word has unique and special meanings for each and every one of us, make sure you word all your important communications carefully, doing everything in your power to make the meaning clear.

Use Mind Maps

Once again, use Mind Maps to help prepare your successful verbal communications. When you have an important letter to write or telephone call to make, do a basic Mind Map® of what you want to say first. This will help you get a clear picture of your goals for the letter or call. It will also allow you to keep track of where you are, to record additional thoughts that may leap into your mind while talking or writing, to be clearer in your message, and, therefore, to feel far more confident in the communication.

In addition to being a tremendous aid in the communication itself, keep the Mind Maps® as a record of the communication. In this way they become a marvellous additional aid to your memory.

Observe Animals Communicating

As you now know, all animals are masterful communicators. Watch animals communicating with humans, with animals of their own kind, and with different animals. Observe the techniques they use for 'checking out others', for making new friends, for 'defending their space' and for getting what they want.

Whenever you see them being successful, check the techniques they used, and wherever you can and wherever appropriate, apply them, to increase your own communication skills as well as your Verbal Intelligence.

Expand Your Professional Vocabulary

One of the most important areas for you to be a communication expert is in your own job. Make a point, every week, of adding new words to your professional vocabulary. This will allow you to communicate more clearly and precisely, and will add significantly to the power your vocabulary gives you in the market place. Remember, the larger your vocabulary the higher your Verbal IQ; the higher your Verbal IQ the more successful you will be; the more successful you are, the more wealthy, in all senses of the word, you become!

Become a Direction Giver

Whenever there is an opportunity for you to help someone by giving directions, leap at it! By incorporating the principles of time, distance, important visual objects and direction, you will help others while, at the same time, developing the precision of your own imagination, the clarity and focus of your words, and your ability to convey any message to anybody. You will guide, in the best sense, other people *and* your own brain towards their desired goals.

Audit Yourself

On a regular basis, perhaps once every three or four weeks, spend a few minutes checking your own progress. Review and order your Verbal Intelligence Knowledge File, checking the number of new words you have acquired. Similarly, check how you are progressing towards your Verbal Intelligence goals; order and, perhaps, adjust your study area, making sure that it is even more inviting to you; and establish your next set of short, medium and long-term goals.

Doing this audit will take very little time. It will keep you constantly aware of the 'Big Picture' IQ development, will reinforce everything you have learnt, will inspire you with confidence, and will motivate and focus you for the continuing work, play and success ahead.

Word Power Booster Number 9

This Word Booster section contains words describing specialists who assist in the maintenance of Physical and Mental Health.

1 OPTICIAN (op-*tí*-shun)
   (a) A technician who grinds lenses
   (b) Eye specialist who fits and prescribes spectacles
   (c) Eye doctor/eye surgeon
   (d) Bone doctor

2 OPTOMETRIST (op-*tóm*-etrist)
   (a) A technician who grinds lenses
   (b) Eye specialist who fits and prescribes spectacles
   (c) Eye doctor/eye surgeon
   (d) Bone doctor

3 OPHTHALMOLOGIST (op-thal-*mól*-ogist)
   (a) A technician who grinds lenses
   (b) Eye specialist who fits and prescribes spectacles
   (c) Eye doctor/eye surgeon
   (d) Bone doctor

4 DERMATOLOGIST (derma-*tól*-ogist)
   (a) Joint doctor
   (b) Bone doctor
   (c) Skin doctor
   (d) Foot doctor

5 PSYCHIATRIST (si-*kía*-trist)

   (a) Doctor who studies general human sickness
   (b) Medical specialist in mental ailments/emotional problems
   (c) One who studies the human mind, its functions and behaviours
   (d) Hypnotist

6 PSYCHOLOGIST (sy-*kólo*-gist)

   (a) Doctor who studies general human sickness
   (b) Medical specialist in mental ailments/emotional problems
   (c) One who studies the human mind, its functions and behaviours
   (d) Hypnotist

7 OSTEOPATH (*ostéo*-path)

   (a) Bone doctor
   (b) Witch doctor
   (c) Ear, eye, nose and throat specialist
   (d) Specialist in ageing

8 PODIATRIST (*pód*-ia-trist)

   (a) Doctor who provides care for pregnant women

   (b) Doctor who specializes in the treatment of very young children

   (c) Doctor who treats minor ailments of the foot

   (d) Nutritional advisor

9 PAEDIATRICIAN (pee-dia-*trí*-shun)

   (a) Doctor who provides care for pregnant women

   (b) Doctor who specializes in the treatment of very young children

   (c) Doctor who treats minor ailments of the foot

   (d) Nutritional advisor

10 OBSTETRICIAN (obste-*trí*-shun)

   (a) Doctor who provides care for pregnant women

   (b) Doctor who specializes in the treatment of very young children

   (c) Doctor who treats minor ailments of the foot

   (d) Nutritional advisor

last words –
using your verbal intelligence
to increase your other multiple intelligences

chapter ten

'Knowledge is power only if it is well organized.'

Tony Buzan

Back in Chapter 1 we learned how our Multiple Intelligences all interact together in synergy. In this chapter we will look briefly at how your massive, and growing Verbal IQ (which is probably now the strongest and most powerful it has ever been in your life) can interweave with just five of these Multiple Intelligences, to the mutual benefit of each!

verbal IQ and creative intelligence

Your Creative Intelligence involves your ability to use your imagination, to make multi-sensory pictures in your mind, to make new and original associations, and to do all this at speed.

Given what you have just learned in *The Power of Verbal Intelligence*, the links between the two are obvious, and by strengthening your Verbal Intelligence you automatically strengthen your imagination, your ability to make new and original associations, and to make multi-sensory pictures in your mind!

And vice versa!

Therefore *use your imagination*! When in conversation, when writing, or when making any form of presentation, *think* about what you are going to say and, very specifically, focus on *imagining* what you are going to say.

For example, if you are describing a meal, infuse it with your imagination. Imagine every molecule of taste and smell; wrap your senses of taste and touch around the texture and delectable flavours of what you are describing; immerse yourself in the wonderful aromas ...

When you do this, you will fire your body with more energy, naturally giving your voice more power, variation, intensity and meaning, and your words an added lustre, beauty and power.

Humour is also a big part of creativity – comedians the world over have proven that the blend of imagination, new and witty associations and words, captivates everyone. Next time you listen to any comedians, analyse their Verbal Intelligence – you will find it is extremely high: their Creative Intelligence will be too!

Mimic them!

As you develop your ability to imagine and make witty new associations, you will be expanding the parameters and power of your Verbal IQ. You will also be enjoying yourself a lot more and gathering many new friends.

verbal IQ and numerical intelligence

Case Study – Word Power = Number Power

What is the relationship between learning mathematics and language skills? A significant one, according to the research of Dr Elizabeth Spelke and Sanna Tsibkin, of the Massachusetts Institute of Technology in Boston.

They studied eight adults who spoke Russian as their native language and who were also fluent in English. To mimic the learning processes of children as they learn mathematics, the researchers taught the subjects both detailed and complex arithmetic, and unfamiliar approximations. To check the relationship between language skills and maths learning, some exercises were taught only in English, the others only in Russian. To make the

using your verbal intelligence to increase your other multiple intelligences

experiment even more language based, the teachers wrote all numbers out as words rather than standard numbers.

The researchers then tested the students by giving them mathematical problems to solve in both languages. They were asked two kinds of questions: first to make exact calculations (does $75 + 89 = 163$ or 164?) and second, to make approximations (is $151 + 95$ closer to 240 or 280?)

The result? In the detailed calculation questions, the students took about a second longer to come up with the answer if the questions were not asked in the language in which they had been taught. This showed a direct relationship between language and ability to learn mathematics.

Interestingly, there was no language-dependent time lag when they were asked to make approximations.

As part of the same study Stanislas Deheene, at the French Medical Research Organization Inserm, watched brain scans of people while they were doing mathematical calculations.

Confirming Spelke and Tsibkin's study, Deheene found that exact calculations increased the activity of speech-related areas of the brain's left-frontal lobe, while estimates increased activity in both the left-and right-parietal lobes. These regions help control hand and finger movements, and perhaps are involved when we learn to count on our fingers.

Your Numerical Intelligence is your ability to juggle successfully in the playground of numbers. It is often mistakenly thought to be not only opposite but counter to Verbal Intelligence. How often do you hear the statement: 'I'm good at maths but hopeless at languages', or 'I love English but hate maths'? The truth of the matter is that both are closely related and each supports the other:

- Both contain basic small alphabets (letters/numbers)
- Both combine the elements of their alphabets to form meaningful sub-groups and larger groups (words/sentences; clusters/equations)
- Each is a prime constituent of standard IQ tests
- Both challenge and stimulate the brain to make associations between their elements
- Both inspire your brain to be creative
- Both have rules and guidelines for their structures; numerical and syntactical 'grammars'
- Both are natural languages
- Both help your brain to refine its processes and to see and think more clearly
- Each is strongly associated with success in academic and business life.

The findings of the case studies above contradict the oft-heard assumptions that if you are good in languages you'll be poor in mathematics and vice versa. If you have a well-developed Verbal

Intelligence, it demonstrably helps you improve your Numerical Intelligence.

You can use your Numerical Intelligence to boost your Verbal IQ in the following two ways:

1. Play games and do puzzles that involve exact calculations. These fun and stimulating games increase the activity of the speech-related areas of your brain. As you entertain yourself in this way you will constantly be exercising the physical areas of your brain that deal with and improve your Verbal Intelligence.

2. Play at describing numerical distances and sizes with words. Try to describe, in words, the following distances (as you describe them, make sure that they are clearly different from each other, and are imaginative in the extreme!):

    - a millimetre
    - a centimetre
    - a metre
    - a kilometre
    - 100 kilometres
    - 1000 kilometres
    - a million kilometres
    - the number 6,000,000,000,
    - the number 1,000,000,000,000
    - infinity

verbal IQ and spatial intelligence

Spatial Intelligence reflects your brain's ability to know and perceive accurately distances and relationships in three-dimensional space.

You have already been introduced to ways your Spatial Intelligence interacts with your Verbal Intelligence – Mind Mapping® and giving people directions!

Use Spatial Intelligence to enhance your Mind Maps®: use *spacing* on the page to indicate close or distant relationships between your words; use word *size* to indicate relative importance; use *dimension* to give emphasis; use *arrows* across the space of the page to show connections; and use *perspective* to show relationships in space.

Use your Spatial Intelligence to help boost your Verbally Intelligent direction-giving skills. Imagine maps or routes around places with which you are familiar, and practise playing through, in your mind's eye, directing someone, in detail, how to get from A to B perfectly. Then put this into practice in real life!

verbal IQ and social intelligence

Social Intelligence refers to your ability to make positive associations on all levels with other human beings. The connections between Social and Verbal Intelligence are plain for all to see.

It is interesting to note that the person with the greatest-ever English vocabulary, Shakespeare (with a massive 25,000 words!) is

---

last words –

using your verbal intelligence to increase your other multiple intelligences

also considered to be the greatest portrayer of the heights (and depths!) of Social Intelligence.

If you are especially interested in this synergetic bond, and its application to your own development, start studying (with simple introductory texts, to guide you) the ultimate master of these two intelligences. You will be well rewarded.

verbal IQ and physical intelligence

Physical Intelligence involves your knowledge and use of your body, the relationship of each part with every other part, and especially its fitness – its poise and posture, aerobic fitness, flexibility, strength, diet and rest. It is intimately associated with your Verbal Intelligence.

When your body is upright and well poised, your entire vocal system (the system that carries and delivers the messages of your Verbal Intelligence) is physically more capable of delivering. The message of your words will also be received far more readily if you are upright and physically congruent, than if you are slouched and off- balance. An excellent postural presence immediately boosts your Verbal Intelligence.

Everyone knows how hard it is to be enthusiastic and sound positive when feeling ill or stressed. Not only that: the quieter and more subdued your speech, the more subdued and 'down' you become!

Get or stay healthy, especially aerobically and flexibly. As with poise/posture, aerobic and flexible fitness have an instantaneous impact on your Verbal Intelligence. The fitter you are, the more energy you will have, and with more energy your words are more affective and memorable.

verbal workout

Word Puzzle Number 19

ginnee	X X __ __ X X
ligboyo	__ X __ X __ X __
litva	__ __ __ __ X
creptiu	__ X X X __ __ X

Clue: Verbal, Creative, Spiritual, Social:

__ __ __ __ __ __ __ __ __ __ __ __

Verbal Intelligence Tip

■ Try unscrambling scrambled words in your head.
Why?
Because unscrambling them in your head is more difficult than jotting them down on paper. By practising this you thus give your verbal muscles an extra strong and good workout. When you are visualizing internally, use all the techniques you have learnt from the previous nine chapters and apply them to your internal visual screen.

By doing this you will also be improving your general brain power, as well as specifically exercising your visualization and Creative Intelligence skills.

Word Puzzle Number 20

Which word completes the phrase?

'A cloud is to rain as lightening is to ...   sky

black

thunder

flash

wind

sun

Word Power Booster Number 10

Your Verbal Intelligence can help you develop insights into others, thus expanding your knowledge of psychology. Your 10 booster words in this section are about the different types of human personality.

1 EFFERVESCENT (effer-*véss*-ent)

(a) Depressed

(b) Bubbling over with energy and enthusiasm

(c) Talkative

(d) Introverted

2 EGOCENTRIC (*égo*-sentrik)

(a) Philanthropic

(b) Inhibited

(c) Self-centred

(d) Solid

3 EGOTIST (ego-*tíst*)

(a) Cheerful person

(b) Shy, reticent, retiring person

(c) Angry person

(d) A conceited, boastful person

4 EXTROVERT (*éxtro*-vert)

(a) Outgoing person

(b) Shy, reticent, retiring person

(c) Angry person

(d) Cheerful person

5 AMBIVERT (*ambí*-vert)

(a) Synonym for extrovert

(b) Shy, reticent, retiring person

(c) Angry person

(d) Combination of extrovert and introvert

6 GREGARIOUS (greg-*ár*-ius)

(a) Introvert

(b) Angry person

---

last words –

using your verbal intelligence to increase your other multiple intelligences

(c) One who loves the company of others

(d) Talkative person

7 QUIXOTIC (*kwíks*-otic)

(a) Knightly

(b) Unreliable

(c) Idealistic but impractical

(d) Lunatic

8 PESSIMIST (*péss*-i-missed)

(a) One who always looks on the dark side of things

(b) One who always looks on the bright side of things

(c) Sarcastic person

(d) Boring person

9 ENTHUSIAST (en*thús*-eeast)

(a) Idealistic but impractical

(b) Saturnine

(c) Egocentric

(d) Person who derives great enjoyment from things

10 OPTIMIST (*optí*-missed)

(a) One who always looks on the dark side of things

(b) One who always looks on the bright side of things

(c) Sarcastic person

(d) Boring person

The last, last word

Congratulations!

You are now a growing member of the worldwide band of graduates of *The Power of Verbal Intelligence*. You are now at the end of your first major journey into the Universe of Verbal Intelligence.

Along this journey you have discovered:

- your Verbal IQ's history and development
- all the 'secret' techniques of that vocabularian genius, the baby
- a fantastic 'Verbal Architect's Kit' of roots, prefixes and suffixes for building infinite improvements in your vocabulary
- an understanding of your brain and its operation, and how to use brain power to increase word power
- a knowledge of your amazing body's amazing body language and how you can improve it
- an awareness and skill in that most important of human arts: becoming a successful and convincing conversationalist and speaker
- an ability to absorb at speed everything from words to entire books
- a new ability to communicate on multi-levels, and
- an awareness of how to use your other incredibly powerful intelligences to maintain and accelerate the growth of your Verbal IQ.

You are ready to take the world by storm!!

Floreant Dendritae! (May your brain cells flourish)
Tony Buzan

Recommended Reading

Tony Buzan's 'Top 10'

The following books and magazines are my own Verbally Intelligent 'Top 10':

1. *The Concise Oxford Dictionary*. This gives you over 240,000 words (10 times Shakespeare's vocabulary!) with meanings, derivations, Roots, Prefixes and Suffixes, and much much more. The ultimate Verbal Intelligence reference book.

2. *Roget's Thesaurus*. The ideal reference book to find words connected by meaning, idea and spirit. A book that will expand your vocabulary, increase your knowledge of simile and metaphor, inspire your creativity, and significantly boost your Verbal IQ.

3. *'Improve Your Vocabulary' books*. There are many of these on the market, and most are valuable. These books guide you through programmed vocabulary power-boosting exercises. Authors particularly recommended are: Dr Wilfred Funk, Ida Ehrlich and Dr Norman Lewis. Alternatively, try some of the many word puzzle, crossword and games magazines that are around: they are guaranteed to exercise and stimulate your Verbal Intelligence!

4. *William Shakespeare*. Any of his works. This supreme master of Verbal, Creative and Social Intelligence is your ideal guide. You may find it is useful to accompany your reading of Shakespeare with study guides to his plays and poetry.

5. *Charles Dickens*. Any of his novels. These stories are delightful to read, and have the added advantage that Dickens loved words, loved playing with them, loved expanding their meanings, and loved using as many different ones as possible. A writer who will stimulate your imagination and power your Verbal Intelligence.

6. *Collected Poems*. Select any volume that contains a wide range of verse from historic to modern. This will allow you to scan the works of some of the great Verbal Intelligences, to be inspired by them and to learn from them.

7. *Get Ahead* by Vanda North. A brain-friendly introduction into the nature of thinking, and how Verbal Intelligence can be blended with your Creative Intelligence to enhance both. An excellent introduction to Mind Maps.

8. *Nurtured by Love* by S. Suzuki. The moving and seminal work by the Japanese genius who demonstrated to the world that our Verbal and Musical Intelligences are infinite.

9. *Teach Your Baby How to Read* by Dr Glen Doman. A book with a similar message to Suzuki's. It will show you the amazing processes by which you learned to read and first develop your Verbal Intelligence, processes which, when you are aware of them, you can continue to use.

10. *The Reader's Digest* magazine. Every month *The Reader's Digest* introduces you to 20 new words in a stimulating two-page section entitled 'It Pays to Increase Your Word Power'. Tens of millions of people (Including me!) have raised their Verbal Intelligence by making this monthly exercise a regular feature of their lives.

Answers

word puzzle answers

Word Puzzle Number 1

1. logic
2. magnify
3. joint
4. eulogy

Answer: Juggling

Word Puzzle Number 2

ass

- lass
- mass
- pass
- glass
- grass
- brass
- bass

Word Puzzle Number 3

1. statue
2. capital
3. clarity
4. bough

Answer: Laughter

Word Puzzle Number 4

end

      tr(**end**)ive = **trend** and **endive**

Word Puzzle Number 5

1. zoology
2. monarch
3. graph
4. connect

Answer: Holanthropy

Word Puzzle Number 6

Knowing

Word Puzzle Number 7

1. deputy
2. creative
3. brains
4. sheikh

Answer: Shakespeare

Word Puzzle Number 8

Philanthropy

Word Puzzle Number 9

1. yacht
2. novel
3. memory
4. idolize

Answer: Leonardo

Word Puzzle Number 10

- Gorennit/Nitrogen
- Mileuh/Helium
- Greti/Tiger
- Nexgyo/Oxygen

Greti/Tiger is the odd one out, as all the rest are gases

Word Puzzle Number 11

1. waltz
2. notify
3. dynamo
4. obvious

Answer: Tony Buzan

Word Puzzle Number 12

Cube. A globe is a three-dimensional circle; a cube is a three-dimensional square.

Word Puzzle Number 13

1. event
2. audio
3. edible
4. quiver

Answer: Eloquent

Word Puzzle Number 14

Holanthropy

Word Puzzle Number 15

1. funny
2. voyage
3. mobile
4. factory

Answer: Vocabulary

Word Puzzle Number 16

Poker

Word Puzzle Number 17

1. prime
2. opera
3. bower
4. knight

Answer: Brain Power

Word Puzzle Number 18

Dual

Word Puzzle Number 19

1. engine
2. biology
3. vital
4. picture
Answer: Intelligence

Word Puzzle Number 20

Thunder – clouds produce rain; lightning produces thunder

word power booster answers

Word Power Booster Number 1

1. (c) To bring in or present
   'I would like to introduce you to my new friend, as I am sure both of you have much in common.'

2. (b) To bend inward
   'We need to introflex the material in order to provide greater stability.'

3. (a) Capable of receiving into itself
   'We need an introceptive object in order to contain this material.'

4. (a) The act of going in; entering
   'In biology, introgression has acquired the specific meaning of transferring genetic information from one species into another.'

5. (d) To throw into
   'I would like to introject some new ideas into this important creative discussion.'

6. (c) To allow to enter; insert (from the Latin '*mittere*', 'to send')
   'We intromit our hands into gloves.'

7. (a) To look within (from the Latin '*specere*', 'to look at')
   'When I examine my own thoughts and feelings I introspect.'

8. (b) To insert (from the zoological term 'intromittent', meaning adapted for insertion)
   'Intromission is necessary if conception is to be achieved.'

9. (a) One who turns inward (from the Latin '*vertere*', 'to turn')
   'He was an introvert, keeping himself to himself, shunning company, and constantly contemplating the meaning of life.'

10. (b) Pressure within (from the Latin 'pressura', 'a pressing')
'His constant worrying resulted in increasing intropression.'

Word Power Booster Number 2

1. (a) Teacher-like; instructive (from the Greek '*didaskein*', 'to teach')
'When explaining things, she had a didactic manner.'

2. (c) Stealthy or secret (from the Latin '*surripere*', 'to steal')
'The surreptitious behaviour going on around him eventually made him feel uneasy.'

3. (d) Revolutionary; contrary to the official/established viewpoint (from the Greek '*hairesis*', 'choice'
'Their heretical beliefs led them into direct conflict with the government, schools and church.'

4. (b) Abundant; plentiful (from the Latin '*copia*', 'plenty')
'After the perfect summer and autumn, with ideal conditions for plants, the abundant harvest yielded a copious supply of fruit, corn and vegetables.'

5. (c) Vital (from the Latin '*imperare*', 'to command')
'It is imperative to upgrade the education system if the nation wishes to be culturally and economically successful.'

6. (b) Incapable of being erased; indelible (from the French *'effacer'*, 'to obliterate')

    'The memories of their time together were so vivid, so wonderful that they could never be destroyed. They were ineffaceable.'

7. (b) Priceless; immeasurable (from the Latin *'aestimare'*, 'to determine, appraise')

    'Despite the attempts of people to price the drawings and paintings of Leonardo, they are of inestimable value.'

8. (a) Never known or done before (from the Latin *'prae'*, 'before' and *'cedere'*, 'to go')

    'The success of the Beatles was an unprecedented musical phenomenon.'

9. (b) Unambiguous; leaving no doubt (from the Latin *'equi'*, 'equally' and *'vocare'*, 'to call')

    'Her statement was so clear; so plain that it was impossible to misunderstand her – it was an unequivocal statement.'

10. (a) Bluntly and unconditionally expressed (from the Greek *'kategorein'*, 'to state, assert')

    'Her statement was categorical; there were no ifs, ands or buts about it – it was absolute.'

Word Power Booster Number 3

1. (d) Fearless (from the Latin 'in', 'not' and 'trepidus', 'fearful, timid')
   'The intrepid explorers faced every obstacle and challenge with not a trace of fear. They were undaunted.'

2. (b) Cannot be taken (from the old French 'prendre', 'to seize or take')
   'The fortress was built to resist any attack; it was built to be impregnable.'

3. (c) Unable to be changed (from the Latin 'in', 'not' and 'alter', 'other')
   'His views on the environment were so much a part of the fabric of his soul that they were unalterable.'

4. (d) Of chief importance (from the old French 'par', 'by' and 'amont', 'above')
   'She said that her family were her main reason for living; they were of paramount importance to her.'

5. (b) Exacting (from the Latin 'rigor', 'stiffness')
   'In order to win five consecutive Olympic Gold Medals, Sir Steve Redgrave participated in one of the most rigorous training programmes imaginable.'

6. (a) Unqualified (from the Latin 'in', 'not' and 'mitigare', 'to soften, alleviate')
   'Because of their rigorous preparation, their cultural tour was an unmitigated success.'

---

7. (c) Reaching the highest point (from the Greek '*klimax*', 'ladder')
    'The climax of her career was receiving the Nobel Peace Prize.'

8. (a) Most sacred; inviolable (from the Latin '*sacer*', 'sacred' and '*sanctus*' / '*sancire*', 'to hallow')
    'His studio was like a temple; no one but himself was allowed in – he considered it sacrosanct.'

9. (c) Unable to be called into question; irreproachable
    'Although Bill Clinton was not impeached, his character is certainly not unimpeachable!'

10. (b) Loud and clear (from the Latin '*clarus*', 'clear')
    'The call to arms was a clarion call for immediate action and mobilization.'

Word Power Booster Number 4

1. (a) Belief that God is non-existent (from the Greek '*a*', 'not' and '*theos*' 'God')
    'By definition no atheist believes in the existence of God!'

2. (b) Uncertainty about God (from the Greek '*a*', 'not' and '*gnostos*', 'known')
    'Agnostics admit that they don't have enough knowledge to decide on whether or not God exists, and consider Atheists too dogmatic.'

3. (c) Generous and unselfish (from the Latin 'alter', 'other')
'Being an altruist she gave generously to charitable causes.'

4. (d) One interested in selfish advantage (from the Latin 'ego', 'I')
'Do egoists normally get along with altruists? Usually no; they are opposites.'

5. (b) One who loves good food; a gourmet (from the Greek philosopher Epicurus, known for his love of the good things in life)
'The Epicure prepared a dinner that was the most fine, aromatic and delicious they had ever had.'

6. (d) One who believes that events are determined by fate (from the Latin 'fatum', 'prediction')
'Because he could not bear the pain of the unfortunate events that had happened to him, he became a fatalist, believing that the Universe had predetermined the events of his life.'

7. (a) A believer in progress (from the Latin 'liber', 'free')
'I am a Liberal. I demand independence in thought and action, and change and experimentation in politics.'

8. (c) A believer in familiar traditions (from the Latin 'conservare', 'to preserve')
'The Conservative wishes to maintain the status quo, and as such is the opposite of the Liberal.'

9. (b) Able to endure pain and hardship without complaining (from the Greek 'stoikos', 'porch'; the Greek philosopher Zeno, the founder of Stoic philosophy, taught at the Stoa Poikile or 'painted porch' in Athens)
'The stoic suffered "the slings and arrows of outrageous fortune" without flinching.'

10. (c) Extreme lover of one's country (from the French aristocrat Nicolas Chauvin of Rochefort, who was over-devoted to Napoleon and France and was ridiculed on the French stage)
'His constant proclamations that his was the only country worthy of any praise on any level identified him as a Chauvinist.'

Word Power Booster Number 5

1. (d) To invest with life
'Our team is looking listless and dull – we need to animate them.'

2. (c) Agreed by all
'The boxer was so superior in his victory the judges gave him a unanimous decision.'

3. (a) Generous and forgiving
'The victor showed great generosity – he was magnanimous in his support and praise of those he had vanquished.'

4. (d) Calmness; composure (from the Latin '*aequus*', 'even' and '*anima*')
   'Despite the frenetic activity going on all around him, he had an aura of complete equanimity.'

5. (c) Turn one's mind to; consider critically (from the Latin '*animus*' and '*advertere*', 'to turn')
   'I animadvert that which I wish to focus.'

6. (b) Important person in industry
   'The magnates, all CEOs of their companies, gathered to celebrate and to discuss creative ideas in business.'

7. (a) Using flowery language
   'He was a magniloquent speaker, embroidering his speech liberally with similes and metaphors.'

8. (b) Greatness; grandeur
   'The magnificence of the new palace dazzled their senses.'

9. (d) Great literary or artistic work
   'Verdi's *Requiem* is considered by many to be his Magnum Opus.'

10. (c) A wine bottle twice the standard size
    'To celebrate their 25th wedding anniversary, they bought themselves a magnum of Champagne.'

Word Power Booster Number 6

1. (c) Hackneyed or stereotyped phrase (from the French '*clicher*', 'to stereotype')
    'His speech was riddled with phrases and sayings that everyone had heard many times before; it was full of clichés.'

2. (b) Comparing one thing with another (from the Latin '*similis*', 'like')
    'When he said that the raging ocean was like a lion, he was using a simile.'

3. (c) Unclear (from the Latin '*ambi*', 'both, around' and '*agere*' 'to lead')
    'His speech was utterly ambiguous, and left everybody completely confused.'

4. (b) A mild word substituted for one that is more direct (from the Greek '*euphemizein*', 'to use auspicious words'; derived from '*eu*', 'good' and '*pheme*', 'speech')
    'Rather than call him "fat", she resorted to euphemism and labelled him "slightly plump".'

5. (a) A conclusion that does not follow from the facts (from the Latin phrase meaning 'it does not follow')
    'He kept on praising her good qualities, and similarly persisted in undermining her thereafter. His conversation was filled with *non sequiturs*.'

the power of verbal intelligence

6. (b) Unnecessary repetition; no longer needed (from the Latin 'redundans', 'overflowing')
   'To describe something as "the littlest, smallest, weeniest, tiniest, microscopic and minimal" is the perfect example of redundancy, and would appear far more appropriately in *Roget's Thesaurus*!'

7. (c) A concise and witty saying (from the Greek '*epigraphein*', 'to write upon')
   'Her speech was dotted with clever, pithy sayings; epigram followed epigram followed epigram.'

8. (c) A word that sounds like what it describes (from the Greek '*onoma*', 'name' and '*poiein*', 'to make')
   '"Buzz"; "sizzle"; and "bong" are all good examples of onomatopoeia.'

9. (a) Light mockery or banter (from the French '*persifler*', 'to tease')
   'The gentleman courteously engaged the young ladies in persiflage.'

10. (b) Something implying a resemblance to something else (from the Greek '*meta*', 'between' and '*pherein*', 'to carry')
   'He felt that "a rabbit caught in the headlights" was a apt metaphor for the hapless goalkeeper.'

Word Power Booster Number 7

1. (c) Speech full of power and imagination
'Soaring flights of imagination and superb diction – his speech was eloquence personified.'

2. (d) Clear and expressive speech
'Professor Higgins' elocution lessons for Eliza Doolittle were, so successful that everyone thought that she was an aristocrat.

3. (b) Talkative; garrulous
'She was loquacious, prattling on virtually non-stop, and far more interested in herself than in what others had to say.'

4. (c) Speaking thoughts aloud when alone; monologue (from the Latin 'solus', 'alone' and 'loqui')
'The soliloquy is one of the main devices by which Shakespeare allows his main characters to reveal their thoughts to the audience.'

5. (b) Using many words when one will do (from the Latin 'circa', 'around' and 'loqui')
'His circumlocution amused those who had been pre-warned that he took an eternity to get to his point.'

6. (d) Conversation; exchange of speech (from the Latin 'inter', 'between' and 'loqui')
'They had an intense and fiery interlocution.'

7. (b) Articulate; inclined to speak
   'People had thought she was shy and disinclined to speak; on the contrary, she was definitely loquent.'

8. (a) A female interlocutor
   'Of the many intelligent women in the group, she was the main interlocutress.'

9. (d) A person's style of speech
   'His locution was characterized by a gentle wit and a large vocabulary.'

10. (c) To declaim; to speak out in public
    'She felt compelled to elocute on the topic of animal welfare.'

Word Power Booster Number 8

1. (a) Love of mankind (from the Greek 'philein', 'to love' and 'anthropos', 'human being')
   'He found human beings so fascinating, he decided to take advanced courses in philanthropy!'

2. (c) Belief in a single supreme deity (from the Greek 'monos', 'one' and 'theos', 'God')
   'Christianity is an example of a religion in which believers practise monotheism.'

3. (b) Hatred of mankind (from the Greek '*misein*', 'to hate' and '*anthropos*', 'human being')
'In his very occasional dark moods the philanthropist occasionally sank into brief bouts of misanthropy.'

4. (c) The love of words and the study of language (from the Greek '*philos*', 'love of' and '*logos*' 'word, knowledge')
'In reading *The Power of Verbal Intelligence* you are engaging in the study of Philology.'

5. (a) The study of the whole human being (from the Greek '*holos*', 'whole' and '*anthropos*', 'human being')
'Rather than studying the human being bit by isolated bit, she decided to study Holanthropy.'

6. (b) Practice of being married to one person at a time (from the Greek '*monos*', 'one' and '*gamos*', 'marriage')
'In most modern societies monogamy is the most common system for marriage.'

7. (c) A tooth with two prongs (from the Latin '*bi*', 'twice' and '*cuspis*', 'point')
'The bicuspid teeth are used more for gripping than chewing.'

8. (b) The study of human history and development
'With our increasing knowledge of the many different tribes and races

that inhabit planet Earth, the study of anthropology has grown in
fascination and stature.'

9. (c) A collector of matchboxes (from the Greek '*philos*', 'love of' and the
    Latin '*lumen*', 'light')
    'When he travelled he kept matchboxes as mementos of some of the
    places he had visited – in the process he became a phillumenist.'

10. (d) One who speaks many languages (from the Greek '*polus*', 'many'
    and '*glotta*', 'tongue')
    'The combination of his constant travels and fascination with different
    languages rapidly evolved him into a polyglot.'

Word Power Booster Number 9

1. (a) A technician who grinds lenses (from the Greek '*optos*', 'seen')
    'In addition to grinding lenses, the optician decided also to sell
    binoculars, telescopes and other optical devices.'

2. (b) Eye specialist who fits and prescribes spectacles
    'The optician became increasingly fascinated with the human eye, and
    decided to increase his knowledge in order to qualify as an
    optometrist.'

3. (c) Eye doctor/eye surgeon (from the Greek '*opthalmos*', 'eye')
    'The optician who had become an optometrist became even more
    fascinated and decided to become a fully-fledged ophthalmologist.'

---

4. (c) Skin doctor (from the Greek 'derma', 'skin')
   'The dermatologist is a specialist in the largest human organ.'

5. (b) Medical specialist in mental ailments/emotional problems (from the Greek 'psukhikos', 'breath, life, soul')
   'She was under incredible mental stress, which gave rise to a plethora of emotional problems. She felt it advisable to seek the advice of a psychiatrist in order to help her through this difficult stage of her life.'

6. (c) One who studies the human mind, its functions and behaviours
   'At an early age she became fascinated by her own and others' behaviours and mental aptitudes; she decided to become a psychologist.'

7. (a) Bone doctor (from the Greek 'osteon', 'bone')
   'Having done his physical workout in a bad mood and while off balance, he ended up with his spine slightly out of alignment. As a result he found himself in the capable hands of an osteopath.'

8. (c) Doctor who treats minor ailments of the foot (from the Greek 'pous', 'foot')
   'He had a pain in his big toe, so decided to go to his podiatrist.'

9. (b) Doctor who specializes in the treatment of very young children (from the Greek 'pais', 'child/boy')
   'Confusing the podiatrist with the paediatrician, the mother mistakenly

the power of verbal intelligence

took her sick infant to the foot doctor!'

10. (a) Doctor who provides care for pregnant women (from the Latin '*obstare*', 'to be present')
'Immediately after she became pregnant, she decided to seek out the best obstetrician available.'

Word Power Booster Number 10

1. (b) Bubbling over with energy and enthusiasm (from the Latin '*effervescere*', 'to boil up')
'Her effervescent personality made her, always, the life and soul of the party.'

2. (c) Self-centred (from the Latin '*ego*', 'I')
'He saw everything from his own point of view; he was insufferably egocentric.'

3. (d) A conceited, boastful person (from the Latin 'ego', 'I')
'He was such an egotist, always boasting about what he had done.'

4. (a) Outgoing person (from the Latin '*extra*', 'outside' and '*vertere*', 'to turn')
'He made friends incredibly easy, having many interests that were "outside himself"– he was a typical extrovert.'

5. (d) Combination of extrovert and introvert (from the Latin 'ambi', 'both')
'He was neither an introvert nor an extrovert; he was a perfectly balanced ambivert.'

6. (c) One who loves the company of others (from the Latin 'grex', 'a flock')
'She was particularly gregarious, always seeking out the company of others.'

7. (c) Idealistic but impractical (from the hero of Cervantes' novel, *Don Quixote*)
'He was a quixotic person, constantly chasing unattainable goals.'

8. (a) One who always looks on the dark side of things (from the Latin 'pessimus', 'the worst')
'No matter how bright the prospects, the pessimist always saw the dark cloud in the silver lining!'

9. (d) Person who derives great enjoyment from things (from the Greek 'entheos', 'inspired')
'It was wonderful to have her at social events – she was such an enthusiast.'

10. (b) One who always looks on the bright side of things (from the Latin 'optimus', 'best')
'The optimist has a particularly positive outlook on the future, always seeing the silver lining in every cloud.'

If you want to learn more about Verbal Intelligence, and to take part in games, quizzes and discussions around all of the subjects covered here, why don't you visit

www.buzancentres.com

or contact Tony at the Buzan Centre:

Buzan Centres Ltd
54 Parkstone Road
Poole, Dorset BH15 2PG
Tel:+44 (0)120 267 4676
Fax:+44 (0)120 267 4776

Buzan Centers Inc. (Americas)
PO Box 4
Palm Beach
FL 33480
Tel:+1 561 881 0188

Or email: buzan@buzancentres.com

Other books by Tony Buzan published by Thorsons:

Head First: 10 Ways to Tap into Your Natural Genius
ISBN 0 7225 4046 9

The Power of Creative Intelligence
ISBN 0 7225 4050 7

The Power of Spiritual Intelligence
ISBN 0 7225 4047 7

Head Strong: How To Get Physically and Mentally Fit
ISBN 0 00 711397 8

Available from all good bookshops, or order direct from HarperCollins
Publishers on:

+44 (0)141 306 3296